In Tribute

Eulogies of Famous People

Ted Tobias

Bushky Press
Beverly Hills, California
2001

BUSHKY PRESS

Published in the United States of America
by Bushky Press
270 N. Canon Dr. #1867
Beverly Hills, California 90210

Originally published in 1999 in a hardcover edition by Scarecrow Press, Inc. under ISBN 0-8108-3537-1
Bushky Press ISBN 0-9711440-0-1

Contents

Preface

The idea for a collection of eulogies came to me the first time I heard Ted Kennedy's voice crack during the last few sentences of his eulogy for his brother, Bobby Kennedy. I visited several public and academic libraries and was surprised that such a collection had seemingly never been published.

After some research I understood why this might be a work of some effort. First I had to formulate a list of the deceased (necrology) to include in the book. This was the easy part: I chose figures from the worlds of government, entertainment, business, sports, and so on. More difficult was to find out whether a eulogy or tribute had been given at the person's funeral and who gave it. The most difficult task was locating the eulogizer (or his or her heir, since many were themselves deceased) and getting permission to include the eulogy in this volume. It took me three years to accumulate all the pieces.

I began my research at public libraries, primarily those in Beverly Hills, California, and UCLA. Necrology books helped extend the list of deceased into the many hundreds. *Who's Who, Who Was Who,* biographies, obituaries, and phone calls to related parties started my list of eulogists.

After locating the desired eulogist or his or her heir, a series of letters was sent detailing the project and requesting permission for the use of the eulogy and also a copy if I did not already have it.

The book is organized alphabetically by the last name of the deceased, and includes biographical sketches of the deceased and their eulogists. There is also an appendix, which alphabetically lists the eulogized, along with their eulogizers, and indexes by eulogist and subject area.

Acknowledgments

My loving wife, Tamar, to whom this book is dedicated, enthusiastically encouraged me to complete the book, just as she has backed me in everything I have ever undertaken.

Thanks to my friend and personal attorney, Barry Rubin, for his help at the very inception.

I am indebted to Rob Gaulin, my New York entertainment lawyer and friend, for his belief in the project, and for his devotion and direction throughout every step along the way. Thanks also to Patti Gaulin and all their staff.

The research and collection of the eulogies could not have been done without my son, Ben, who did the major part of the library research, and my daughter, Leora who handled most of the processing and contact work. I thank them both.

A special thanks to the staff at Sterling Typography, in Hawthorne, California, for their typing of the entire book, especially owner Valerie Cissell, Bernard Brandt, and Michael Carney.

Special thanks also are due to my dear friends, Arlene and the late Danny Dayton, for their suggestions and introductions.

I extend my appreciation to the countless librarians and personal assistants to the eulogizers who took the time to help locate many of the materials.

Permission for each eulogy in this book was obtained from either the person delivering the eulogy or a relative or representative of that person. The eulogy for David Niven, which originally appeared in the *National Review* on August 19, 1983, is copyrighted by NATIONAL REVIEW, Inc. 215 Lexington Ave., New York, NY 10016, and is reprinted by permission.

Front cover photos © Hulton Archives.

Tobias photo by Jeff Knight, www.heatshotetc.com.

Louis Armstrong

July 4, 1900 ~ July 6, 1971

Tribute by Congressman Charles B. Rangel,
given in the Congress and appearing
as part of the *Congressional Record*

Louis Armstrong

Musician Louis ("Satchmo," "Pops") Armstrong was born in New Orleans to Willie and Mary-Ann Armstrong. He married Daisy Parker in 1917, from whom he later was divorced. In February 1924 he married Lillian Hardin. After another divorce, he married his third wife, Lucille, in 1942. A lifelong musician who began by playing the bugle, Armstrong became a clarinetist and trumpeter as well as a singer, composer, orchestra leader, and recording artist.

Armstrong's professional career began with King Ory's band in 1917, after which, in 1922, he became a cornetist with Joe (King) Oliver in Chicago. He abandoned the clarinet for the trumpet in 1925. His recording "You Rascal" scored a hit in England, and after touring the United States with his band, he appeared in London at the Palladium, during the first of what would be many international tours.

Armstrong was the composer of many well-known songs, including "Where Did You Stay Last Night," "Satchel Mouth Swing," and "I've Got a Heart Full of Rhythm." He appeared in several motion pictures, including *Every Day's a Holiday* (1938), *Going Places* (1938), *Cabin in the Sky* (1943), the *Glenn Miller Story* (1953), *High Society* (1956), and *The Five Pennies* (1959). His recordings number about fifteen hundred, many being valued as collector's items.

Louis Armstrong was named Number One Male Singer by the Sixteenth International Jazz Critics Poll in 1968. He was also honored by the Jazz and Pop Third Annual Readers' Poll. Armstrong was a member of ASCAP.

Charles B. Rangel

Congressman Charles Bernard Rangel was born in Harlem, New York, on June 11, 1930, the son of Ralph and Blanche (Wharton) Rangel. He married Alma Carter in 1961, and the couple have two children. Rangel earned a B.S. from New York University in 1957 and was granted a J.D. from St. John's University School of Law in 1960. He has, in addition, received awards and honorary degrees from various academic institutions, including Wagner College, Atlanta University, New York University, Howard University, and Hofstra. He joined the New York Bar in 1963.

Assistant U.S. attorney for the southern district of New York from 1961 to 1962, Rangel has been a member of the New York State Assembly since 1966. He has served the 92d through 103d Congresses in Washington, D.C., as representative from the Nineteenth (now the Fifteenth) New York District from 1971 to the present. In this latter capacity he has been a member of the House Ways and Means Committee and a member of the Joint Committee on Taxation.

He served with the United States Army from 1948 to 1952 in Korea. Rangel has been decorated with the Bronze Star and the Purple Heart, and was awarded a Korean Presidential Citation.

Congressman Rangel was a close friend of Louis Armstrong.

Tribute for Louis Armstrong by Congressman Charles B. Rangel

Louis (Satchmo) Armstrong once pointedly stated—"Either you got it or you ain't."

And as the master showman, Satchmo certainly had it. We all recall that deep guttural voice, that grin as wide as a keyboard, and that horn which blew sweet and clear.

On July 6, Satchmo suddenly left us. He died in his sleep of heart failure shortly after observing his seventy-first birthday. I was in the process of drafting legislation to honor his enormous contribution to music, when I learned of his death.

He will always remain in my mind as one of the main forces in the development of jazz that helped shape it into the great musical form it is today.

I am proud to have introduced with the support of my fifty-three colleagues legislation to provide that a gold medal be presented to the widow of the late Louis Armstrong in recognition of Mr. Armstrong's contributions in the field of music and in recognition of his great achievement as a goodwill ambassador abroad for the United States.

The legislation authorizes the secretary of the treasury to strike a gold medal with suitable inscriptions.

He was a marvelous storyteller. He had a funny story about anything and everything and everybody! You could give him any subject, or mention a name, and he'd unreel a story that would have you rolling on the floor. Anyone who knew him has his own favorite that Pops has told him.

And with it all, in this amazing career that spanned fifty-five years, and brought him such continuous universal recognition and honor and fame, he was basically a modest, unpretentious, simple man, devoted to his wonderful wife, Lucille, who gave him thirty years of great happiness, his home here in Corona, and his friends and neighbors.

His credo was simple: "I never tried to prove nothing, just always wanted to give a good show. My life has been my music, it's always come first, but the music ain't worth nothing if you can't lay it on the public. The main thing is to live for that audience, 'cause what you're there for is to please the people."

Well, he pleased the people alright! More than that, Louis Armstrong captured the essence of human relations in what he did. . . . The feeling, the mood, the spirit, the hope of mankind.

So, move over, Gabriel, 'cause here comes "Satchmo" and "The saints are marching in!!" And so "Pops" takes his place as the "King" . . . at the head of that big jam session in the sky, in that special niche in heaven that God keeps to hold our idols. . . . With Billie, and Fats, and Johnny Hodges, and Bird . . . with Tommy and Jimmy and Bessie . . . and Big Sid . . . and Ziggy, and Jack Teagarden, and Bunny . . . with Edmund Hall, and Billy Kyle, and Pee Wee Russell, and Dinah and Velma, and Sidney Bechet. . . . With Davey Tough and Mildred Bailey, and Coleman Hawkins, and Ben Webster . . . with Nat Cole and Claude Thornhill . . . and Jimmy Lunceford . . . Glenn Miller and Wes Montgomery, and Tad Dameron and Bud Powell, Charley Shavers, and on, and on, and on.

Louis Armstrong was a lovable, beautiful, darling man . . . with a beautiful soul. He loved all kinds of people, and all kinds of people loved him. He had a full, rich, rewarding life. It was an epic! . . . And he had a ball!! He spread a lot of sunshine around and all those he touched are richer for it, and the world is a whole lot better for his having been in it.

For as long as there are ears to hear, his music will be played and enjoyed and studied . . . and he will endure.

He was truly the only one of his kind, a titanic figure of his and our time . . . a veritable Picasso, a Stravinsky, a Casals . . . a Louis Armstrong. In his musical autobiography, writer Gilbert Millstein quotes seven lines from a novel called *The Circus of Dr. Lao* by Charles Finney, which fit Louis's life perfectly:

> For he wanted to make one hell of a show,
> And the things you'll see in your brains will glow
> Long past the time when the winter snow
> Has frozen the summer's furbelow.
> For this is the circus of Dr. Lao . . .
> And youth may come and age may go;
> But no more circuses like this show!

It *was* one hell of a show! Goodbye, Pops!

Arthur Ashe

July 10, 1943 ~ February 6, 1993

Eulogy delivered by Governor L. Douglas Wilder
at a memorial service, Arthur Ashe Center,
Richmond, Virginia, February 10, 1993

Arthur Ashe

American tennis player Arthur Robert Ashe Jr. was born in Richmond, Virginia, the son of Arthur Robert and Mattie C. (Cunningham) Ashe. He married Jeanne-Marie Moutoussamy in February 1977, and the couple had one child. Ashe received a B.S. in business administration from UCLA in 1966.

The winner of two U.S. intercollegiate championships during college, Ashe won the U.S. Men's Hard Court Championship in 1963, the U.S. Men's Clay Court (1967), and the U.S. Amateur title (1968). In 1968 he won the U.S. men's singles and Open championships, and the Australian Open in 1970. Ashe went on to win the French Open doubles (1972), the Wimbledon singles (1975), and the World Championship Tennis singles (1975). Ashe was a member of the U.S. Davis Cup Team for ten years, and its captain in 1981.

In 1979, a heart attack forced Ashe to retire from his tennis career, and he turned his energy to social activism. Among his concerns were South African apartheid and Haitian refugees. He was also active in many public health organizations.

Ashe was a member of the board of directors of Aetna Life and Casualty, and in 1973 authored the book *Portrait in Motion* with Frank DeFord. In 1981 he wrote *Off the Court* (with Neil Amdur), and *A Hard Road to Glory* (1988). Ashe served as the campaign chairman for the American Heart Association from 1981 to 1982.

L. Douglas Wilder

Lawrence Douglas Wilder was born in the Church Hill section of Richmond along with six sisters and a brother. In 1951, after graduating from Virginia Union University in Richmond with a B.S. in chemistry, Wilder joined the U.S. Army. While serving in Korea, he received the Bronze Star.

Upon his return to Virginia, Wilder worked as a chemist for the state medical examiner's office. When he decided to take advantage of the GI Bill to study law, he had to go out of state, as Virginia barred blacks from attending its law schools at that time. In 1959, he received a J.D. degree from Howard University School of Law in Washington, D.C. After passing the bar, he established the law firm that came to be known as Wilder, Gregory and Associates—one of the few minority-owned businesses in Virginia—and went on to develop a reputation as a top criminal trial lawyer.

Wilder entered politics in 1969 as a state senator in Virginia. During his five terms he chaired committees on transportation, rehabilitation, and social services. He also served on the Virginia Advisory Legislative Council, on the Democratic Steering Committee, and as Virginia's lieutenant governor.

On January 13, 1990, Wilder was sworn in as Virginia's sixty-fifth governor—the first African-American governor in U.S. history. That he was elected in the former capital of the Confederacy that had once denied him admission to its white-only schools made the event even more significant.

L. Douglas Wilder and Arthur Ashe were longtime friends.

Eulogy for Arthur Ashe by Governor L. Douglas Wilder

I know that I speak for a great number of Virginians who thank all of Arthur's friends from so many places who've come to say to the family how much we love him and feel about this great Virginian, this great American.

You know you usually ask the question when someone has passed: "What were you doing at that time?" And usually there's some kaleidoscopic occurrence in your mind that makes you recall, "I was doing this or that." It was quite the reverse with me with Arthur.

I have always remembered when I first met him, and that image has always stayed with me: Practicing playing tennis—by himself. And for those who knew him, they know that he was not a lonely man. And he always belonged to all of us. But that image said so much of him: solitary and proud and determined.

He was never lonely. No man ever treasured friendship and family more than Arthur. And no one has been more open to others. He had a quiet soul amid a very busy and noisy life. And he lived in such a way and he carried that grace and dignity with such aplomb that he served as a model for so many people. Not (just) youngsters, but so many of us.

Oh, I think he would have preferred mightily to have been known as a great tennis player—not as a great black tennis player. I think he would have preferred to have been known as one who was concerned with his fellow man, and in fact (he was).

His fate touched him with greatness, and he showed that he would never shrink from his responsibility and the life that followed.

I've read on occasions that some had said he expressed resentment and bitterness about his hometown—Richmond, Virginia. And yet I've never heard him express that with me.

Oh, we all expressed our resentment against the status quo. . . . He had his reasons why he didn't. And those of you (especially his colleagues in the tennis world)—when you came here with him, you saw the accolades, the crowds, the people who adored him and adulated him even then. And yet those of us who remember, remember a composed athlete.

We know (his composure) even when the umpires were wrong. Clearly so. He didn't berate them.

He knew what it meant to have to be better.

He knew that the standards would be higher.

He knew that the calls sometimes would be against him when all the world knew they shouldn't have been.

But he said nevertheless, "I'll be a champion." And he was.

And he used every fiber of his strength on and off the court to right the world's injustices.

Oh, he didn't seek the counsel of what was popular, nor did he concern himself with plaudits or approvals.

He made up his mind, kept his own countenance, and (practiced) the discipline we've all come to know. And he did what he set out to do.

> Though wise men at their end know dark is right,
> because their words had forked no lightning, they
> do not go gentle into that good night. . . .
> Rage, rage against the dying of the light.

And he raged against the cards that were dealt in the latter stages of his life. He determined that he would not let even that deter or to stop him from that indefatigable job that obviously he was chosen by fate to perform. And that is the spreading of human kindness and loving kindness.

Oh, to be with the youngsters when they would come up and grab his hand—and look at him with awe and wonder and say, "If he did it, I can, too." And that was his message: "If I can do it, you can do it." And he did so with a quiet peace and dignity that gave every utterance (the sense) that he was at peace at all times.

> You know it is said there are ten strong things.
> That iron is strong, but fire melts it . . .
> That fire is strong, but water puts it out . . .
> That water is strong, but the clouds evaporate it . . .
> That the clouds are strong, but the wind blows them away . . .
> That man is strong, but fear is stronger . . .
> That fear is strong, but wine allays it . . .
> That wine is strong, but sleep overcomes it . . .
> That sleep is strong, but death far stronger . . .
> But loving kindness survives even death.

George Burns

January 20, 1896 ~ March 9, 1996

Eulogy delivered by Irving Fein at the funeral
in Los Angeles, California

George Burns

Actor-comedian George Burns (originally Nathan Birnbaum) was born in New York City. In January 1926, he married fellow entertainer Gracie Allen, and the couple had two children.

Burns began his professional career as a dancer in vaudeville, and first teamed with Allen in 1923. He became her straight man, playing the confused husband to Allen's daffy wife. They worked together in radio from 1932 until 1950, when they moved to television with their popular series, *The Burns and Allen Show,* which ran until Allen's retirement in 1958.

A master of the one-liner, Burns continued to work into his nineties as a stand-up comedian, actor, and TV personality. In 1975, he was awarded the Oscar for best supporting actor for *The Sunshine Boys.* His other films include *Oh God!* (1977), *Oh God! Book Two* (1980), and *Oh God! You Devil* (1984).

Burns was also the author of several books, including *Living It Up, or, They Still Love Me in Altoona* (1976), *How to Live to Be One Hundred or More* (1983), and *Wisdom of the '90s* (1991). In 1988, Burns was a recipient of the Kennedy Center Honor for his contributions to U.S. cultural life. He was one hundred years old at the time of his death in 1996.

Irving Fein

Television and motion picture executive Irving Ashley Fein was born in Brooklyn on June 21, 1911, the son of Harry and Fannie (Milstein) Fein. He attended the University of Baltimore from 1928 to 1929, and the University of Wisconsin from 1930 to 1932. In 1936 he was granted an LL.B. from St. Lawrence University in Canton, New York. After the death of his first wife, Florence Kohn, Fein married Shepard Schechter in 1969.

Fein joined the publicity and advertizing department of Warner Brothers in New York City in 1933, and later became its director of exploitation and radio on the West Coast. In 1941, he was appointed the assistant publicity director for Samuel Goldwyn, and the following year moved to Columbia Pictures as their director of exploitation. He continued his work in public relations for CBS Radio throughout the 1950s. From 1956 to 1966, he was the president of J. & M. Productions, Inc., of Beverly Hills, and was also the executive vice president of JAC Productions until 1975. During this time, he produced programs for such entertainers as Jack Benny, and was the producer of George Burns's TV specials from 1975 until Burns's death in 1996.

Fein produced such films as *Just You and Me, Kid* (1979), and *Oh God! You Devil* (1984). Irving Fein received an Emmy award in 1961, and in 1976 wrote *Jack Benny: An Intimate Biography*.

Irving Fein and George Burns were friends for over fifty years, and Fein represented Burns as his manager for over twenty years. Fein currently resides in Beverly Hills, California.

Eulogy for George Burns by Irving Fein

Today we are here to pay our respects to one of the most beloved performers of the show business world. Everyone here knew him so long that there is very little I can say about this remarkable man that you don't already know. Singer . . . dancer . . . straight man . . . actor . . . comedian . . . author. He will leave a very large void in our lives. I knew George for fifty years and had the happy privilege of representing him for the last twenty-two; and until he fell in 1994, what *marvelous* years they were.

One of the many things I admired about George was his absolute determination to keep doing what he loved best in the world: working in show business. Always on time (or early), always prepared, he never missed a single performance and was the consummate professional. And as the years advanced, and I would discuss his possible retirement, he would say, "Retire? What am I supposed to do, stay home and play with my cuticles?" Or he'd say, "Quit? I can't quit. Who would support my mother and father?" It was that attitude, plus his many gifts, plus the love from his adoring fans coming across the footlights wherever he worked, that enabled him to stay on top all those years.

George always gave Gracie credit for their success on stage. But he was the one who knew what would or wouldn't work. As he often said, he knew entrances and exits. And last Saturday, he knew it was time to go.

He was here for one hundred great years. We may have wished for more but no one in this room could have wanted him to just hang on, unable to hear the laughter and applause, or take his bows.

So George, we'll miss you. I know you took your music with you, so wherever you are, I hope they're playing it in your key.

Cesar Chavez

March 31, 1927 ~ April 23, 1993

Homily delivered by Cardinal Roger Mahony at the funeral mass, Forty Acres, Delano, California, April 29, 1993

Cesar Chavez

American labor leader Cesar Estrada Chavez was born in Yuma, Arizona, the son of a migrant farm worker. He married Helen Favila, and the couple had eight children. From 1952 to 1962 Cesar Chavez worked with the Community Service Organization (CSO),which helped poor communities organize themselves into more powerful blocs. While with the CSO, Chavez registered Mexican American voters and aided in solving their problems with government agencies. He became the general director in 1958.

Cesar began organizing farm workers, and in 1962 founded the United Farm Workers (UFW). In the mid-sixties, Chavez worked with the AFL-CIO in a strike against vineyard owners in an attempt to bring pressure on California growers to sign union contracts with the UFW. He dramatized the struggle by initiating the first of his many fasts. Chavez and the UFW were later undermined when the Teamsters' Union began to organize farm workers. In March of 1977, the two unions agreed that the UFW would have jurisdiction over field workers, and that the Teamsters would restrict its activities to truck drivers and cannery workers. In 1988, Chavez promoted a grape and lettuce boycott during a thirty-six- day fast.

Chavez was president of the United Farm Workers until his death at age sixty-six. He is recognized as one of the preeminent Hispanic American leaders of our time.

Cardinal Roger Mahony

Cardinal Archbishop Roger M. Mahony was born in Hollywood, California, on February 27, 1936, the son of Victor James and Loretta Marie (Baron) Mahony. He was granted an A.A. from Our Lady Queen of Angels Seminary in 1956, and a B.A. from St. John's Seminary College in 1958. He earned a bachelor of sacred theology degree in 1962 and master's in social work in 1964 from the Catholic University of America in Washington, D.C. Mahony was ordained a Roman Catholic priest in 1962, a bishop in 1975, and a cardinal priest in 1991.

From 1968 to 1973 he served as assistant pastor of St. John's Cathedral in Fresno, and was its rector from 1973 to 1980. During the 1960s, Mahony resided at St. Genevieve's Parish in Fresno, first as administrator and then as pastor. During this period, Mahony was named chancellor of the diocese of Fresno (1970), and served as its vicar general and auxiliary bishop (1975 to 1980). He was bishop of the diocese of Stockton, California, from 1980 to 1985. Mahony became archbishop of the Archdiocese of Los Angeles in 1985, and was proclaimed its cardinal in 1991.

Well known for his stands on social justice issues, and pastoring U.S. Catholicism's largest Chicano population, Mahony was the director of the Catholic Welfare bureau from 1964 to 1970, and is a member of the Canon Law Society of America and the National Association of Social Workers.

Cardinal Mahony was a longtime supporter of Cesar Chavez, and a personal friend.

Eulogy for Cesar Chavez by Cardinal Mahony

The incredible energy of today's Scriptures captivates us as we listen to the letter from James and the Gospel from Matthew, as our hearts and minds resonate with the wondrous strength of God calling all of us to live as instruments for justice, respecters of human rights and dignity for all peoples, guarantors of economic rights for the farm workers and laborers of the world, and peacemakers.

The challenge of these Scriptures surrounds us as we gather with our many different stories that have linked each of us with Cesar Chavez and with his charismatic leadership over the past decades. Each person here can relate his or her own story about when, where, and how they first met Cesar; how his influence helped to shape their lives and destinies; and how their own commitment to seek a new dignity and economic justice for all farm workers was sparked in their lives by Cesar.

The simple energy of these two Scriptures served as a spiritual foundation for Cesar, and they nourished him as a disciple of Jesus Christ, as one who believed in the promises of Christ, and one who hoped in the power of the Lord's Resurrection. In their own way, James's letter and

Jesus' Sermon on the Mount are like the spiritual idealism that so motivated Cesar throughout his life with the stark realism of the struggle for farm workers' rights, dignity, and justice that won the supreme commitment of his entire life.

In James's letter to the early Church, he castigates and condemns those rich people who have amassed this world's goods through the sweat, labors, heartaches, and deprivations of the poor and their families. In some of the strongest language found in the Scriptures, James scolds those wealthy people who have become rich by withholding the just wages of their farm workers. He assures those deprived workers that their cries have been lifted up to the ears of the Lord of hosts and have been heard.

James, like all God's prophets before him, understood his mission as proclaiming forthrightly God's vision and design for the human family, and to call all peoples to transform their lives to reflect that design. So, too, did Cesar accept his role as a special prophet for the world's farm workers. Faithful to this call, Cesar Chavez dedicated himself:

To serve as a special champion for the poor, the migrant, the ones who toiled in the fields that put food on the nation's tables;

To serve as a promoter of God's plan that extends to all people, regardless of race, language, or occupation;

To serve as prophet who was bold enough to criticize and to energize, to proclaim the vision of justice embodied in God's kingdom and to denounce unjust systems that withheld wages or defrauded farm workers and their families;

To serve as the keeper of this sacred vision, constantly reminding farm workers of their just goals;

To serve as the prophet who could imagine and envision a future in which farm workers were treated with dignity and justice, and to empower farm worker mothers and fathers to pass on that dream, that vision, to their own children.

Cesar Chavez, like James, embraced the true prophet's role as he gave personal witness to the power of God's grace in his life, and as he instilled hope in thousands of farm workers across the nation. True to the prophetic role:

Cesar waged a relentless fight to promote the dignity of the farm worker and of farm worker families;

Cesar battled against decades-old unjust systems to ensure that farm workers' basic rights to a living wage, to safe working conditions, to decent housing, to health care, and to their children's education were guaranteed;

Cesar recognized early on that it was only in and through the "community"—of families and of farm workers united—that any lasting systemic change could occur;

Cesar's personal commitment to farm workers is best summarized by his dedication to walk with and accompany his poor brothers and sisters, the vulnerable, and the voiceless, the unorganized, on their journeys towards justice;

Cesar was willing to physically put himself in the middle of these struggles: whether it was on the picket lines facing possible violent retribution; or fasting to ground himself spiritually and emotionally for his prophetic work; or on the endless days and nights of speeches and rallies in church basements, homes of supporters, or in the fields with the farm workers whom he knew and loved.

Jesus' Sermon on the Mount captures and rivets our attention today because of its obvious comparison to the struggles of today's poor, powerless, disenfranchised, and our nation's farm workers. Likewise, this sermon points to the prophetic role lived out by Cesar Chavez. Permit me to rephrase those Beatitudes to reflect in a contemporary fashion both the struggle of farm workers, and their resultant blessing by God.

How blest are the poor, God's *anawim,* our nation's farm worker families, whose poverty is real and economic: God's grace is poured out into their lives, and God's Kingdom is theirs!

Blest, too, are so many farm workers who suffer the trials of hard work, frequent injuries, the punishment of the blazing sun, and the harmful results of farm chemicals: God will heal their bodies and console their agonies and sorrows through the power of His Resurrection!

Blest are those who toil daily in the fields, but who are slow to anger, gentle with others, and patient in hardship: God will reward them with the hills, the fields, and the lands of the earth!

Best are the farm worker artisans of peace and the doers of justice: God shall call them His sons and daughters, and give them Our Lady of Guadalupe as their Mother!

Blest are you when they insult you and persecute you through inadequate justice systems, unequal application of the law, discrimination and harassment: God will reward you with His justice and peace on this earth, and the fullness of life in heaven!

As we have listened to the messianic manifesto of Jesus Christ as proclaimed in the Sermon on the Mount, we have come to realize ever more deeply how immense is God's love for the poor, but how fleeting is His patience with those who practice injustice.

Cesar Chavez understood fully the depth of God's love, and never hesitated for a moment to proclaim that same messianic manifesto of Christ. Like those great prophets of times past, Cesar Chavez found a closeness to God and an inner peace on a mountain. "La Paz" in the Tehachapi mountains invigorated his spirit and energized his vision.

Cesar Chavez lived deeply his faith in God and his commitment to the Body of Christ, the Church. He knew well the value of popular religiosity and its wondrous effect upon farm workers. Unafraid to witness his faith publicly, the ever-present banner of Our Lady of Guadalupe preceded every march, every rally, and every union demonstration.

Cesar loved the many Spanish acclamations that are so much a part of the spiritual legacy of the people: ¡Viva Cristo Rey! ¡Viva Nuestra Señora de Guadalupe!—and others. And to this list he added the ever-popular expression of faith: ¡Sí, se puede!

Throughout Mexico and Latin America there is a beautiful custom when the community mourns the death of their special leaders who fought long and hard for a more just society. They recite a litany of names of men and women, laypersons, priests, and religious women who have given their lives for the cause of justice and peace. The response to each name brings a rousing response from the community of "Presente."

This response of "Presente" symbolizes most vividly the way in which the spirit of those individuals continues to thrive in the community, and the commitment of the community to continue the struggle which those leaders' lives embodied.

Today we celebrate the fullness of Cesar's life. But we also celebrate a renewed commitment to embrace the values he held so dear and for which he was unwilling to compromise. To the longtime cry of "¡Huelga!" we must now add "¡Presente!" as we continue forward with the work that Cesar initiated over thirty years ago.

As we celebrate this Eucharist of the new life in Christ, of new hope in the power of God's grace, and of our renewed dedication to the works of justice and peace for all farm workers and their families, we now add to that special litany of prophetic heroes: Cesar Chavez, and we all respond with faith and with fervor: "Presente."

Sir Winston Churchill

November 30, 1874 ~ January 24, 1965

Eulogy delivered by Dwight D. Eisenhower, St. Paul's Cathedral, London, England, January 30, 1965

Sir Winston Churchill

English statesman Sir Winston Leonard Spencer Churchill, the eldest son of Lord Randolph Churchill, was born at Blenheim Palace, Woodstock, Oxfordshire, England, and educated at Harrow and the Royal Military College at Sandhurst. He served with the 1898 Nile expeditionary force, fighting hand-to-hand against the Dervishes at Omdurman. While covering the Boer War for a London newspaper, he was captured in an ambush in 1899, but successfully escaped.

In 1900, he was elected to Parliament as a Conservative, but his differences with the party widened and he joined the Liberals in 1906, becoming colonial undersecretary. From 1908 to 1910 he served in the Cabinet as president of the Board of Trade. He was appointed home secretary in 1910, and in the following year, as the "father of naval aviation," he prepared the Royal Navy for the war he foresaw.

In 1915, he was made the scapegoat for the Dardanelles disaster and joined the army in France. In 1917, he became David Lloyd George's minister of munitions. From 1919 to 1921, he was secretary of state for war and air, and in 1924 he was appointed Chancellor of the Exchequer in Stanley Baldwin's Conservative government (1924 to 1929). Between 1929 and 1939, Churchill did not hold office. As World War II drew closer, he warned against the growing threat of Nazi Germany, urging the British government to match Germany's prowess.

When war came he was back at the Admiralty. When power slipped from the hands of Neville Chamberlain in 1940, Churchill formed a Coalition government and began his "walk with destiny." Offering the British people nothing but "blood, toil, tears and sweat," his voice incomparably expressed the national spirit of resistance. Churchill gave highest priority to battling German U-boats and repelling the Luftwaffe assault on Britain. He was on close personal terms with President Franklin Roosevelt, and sustained an often difficult alliance with the Soviet Union.

Defeated in the July 1945 election at the height of his wartime fame, he became a pugnacious leader of the opposition. In international speeches he warned about the tyranny behind the Iron Curtain and fostered the conception of European and Atlantic unity, later to bear fruit in NATO and other supranational organizations. In 1951, at the age of seventy-seven, he became prime minister again. When he resigned his office in 1955, he was the last surviving member of the Allied triumvirate.

Although weaker in health, Churchill's final ten years were occupied by travel, painting, and writing. He was awarded the Nobel Prize for literature in 1953 and received an honorary United States citizenship in 1963, at that time the only one given. Upon his death in 1965 he was ninety years old.

Dwight D. Eisenhower

For a biographical sketch, see the eulogy for Dwight D. Eisenhower, page 27. Eisenhower served closely with Winston Churchill in the Allied Forces Command during World War II.

Eulogy for Sir Winston Churchill by Dwight D. Eisenhower

Upon the mighty Thames, a great avenue of history, move at this moment to their final resting place the mortal remains of Sir Winston Churchill. He was a great maker of history, but his work done, the record closed, we can almost hear him, with the poet, say:

> Sunset and evening star,
> And one clear call for me!
> Twilight and evening bell
> And after that the dark!
> And may there be no sadness of farewell,
> When I embark.

As I, like all other free men, pause to pay a personal tribute to the giant who now passes from among us, I have no charter to speak for my countrymen—only for myself. But, if in memory, we journey back two decades to the time when America and Britain stood shoulder to shoulder in global conflict against tyranny, then I can presume—with propriety, I think—to act as spokesman for the millions of Americans who served with me and their British comrades during three years of war in this sector of the earth.

To those men Winston Churchill was Britain—he was the embodiment of British defiance to threat, her courage in adversity, her calmness in danger, her moderation in success. Among the Allies his name was spoken with respect, admiration, and affection. Although they loved to chuckle at his foibles, they knew he was a staunch friend. They felt his inspirational leadership. They counted him a fighter in their ranks.

The loyalty that the fighting forces of many nations here serving gave to him during that war was no less strong, no less freely given, than he had, in such full measure, from his own countrymen.

An American, I was one of those Allies. During those dramatic months, I was privileged to meet, to talk, to plan, and to work with him for common goals.

Out of that association an abiding—and to me precious—friendship was forged; it withstood the trials and frictions inescapable among men of strong convictions, living in the atmosphere of war.

The war ended, our friendship flowered in the later and more subtle tests imposed by international politics. Then, each of us, holding high official posts in his own nation, strove together so to concert the strength of our two peoples that liberty might be preserved among men and the security of the free world wholly sustained.

Through a career during which personal victories alternated with defeats, glittering praise with bitter criticism, intense public activity with periods of semiretirement, Winston Churchill lived out his four score and ten years.

With no thought of the length of the time he might be permitted on earth, he was concerned only with the quality of the service he could render to his nation and to humanity. Though he had no fear of death, he coveted always the opportunity to continue that service.

At this moment, as our hearts stand at attention, we say our affectionate, though sad, goodbye to the leader to whom the entire body of free men owes so much.

In the coming years, many in countless words will strive to interpret the motives, describe the accomplishments, and extol the virtues of Winston Churchill—soldier, statesman, and citizen that two great countries were proud to claim as their own. Among all the things so written or spoken, there will ring out through all the centuries one incontestable refrain: Here was a champion of freedom.

May God grant that we—and the generations who will remember him—heed the lessons he taught us: in his deeds, in his words, in his life.

May we carry on his work until no nation lies in captivity; no man is denied opportunity for fulfillment.

And now, to you Sir Winston—my old friend—farewell!

John Connally

February 27, 1917 ~ June 15, 1993

Eulogy delivered by Lady Bird Johnson, June 17, 1993

John Connally

John B. Connally III was born in Floresville, Texas, the son of John Bowden and Lela Connally. He received both his bachelor's and his J.D. degrees from the University of Texas. Originally a Democrat, Connally served as President John F. Kennedy's secretary of the navy from 1961 to 1962, and was governor of Texas from 1963 to 1969. In 1963, he was riding in President Kennedy's car in Dallas when Kennedy was assassinated; Connally was seriously wounded.

From 1971 to 1972 he served as Richard Nixon's secretary of the treasury, and in 1972 worked in Nixon's reelection campaign. Connally joined the Republican party and briefly campaigned for the 1980 presidential nomination before deferring to Ronald Reagan.

Although Connally had become wealthy from oil and real estate investments, by the late 1980s he had overextended himself and declared bankruptcy, selling off almost his entire two-thousand-plus-acre ranch. Connally died in Houston at age seventy-six.

Lady Bird Johnson

Lady Bird (Mrs. Lyndon Baines) Johnson was born Claudia Alta Taylor in Karnack, Texas, on December 22, 1912. At the University of Texas she received a bachelor of arts (1933), a bachelor of journalism (1934), and a doctorate in law (1964). On November 17, 1934, she married Lyndon Baines Johnson, and together the couple had two children, Lynda Bird and Lucy Baines.

From 1941 to 1942, Lady Bird managed her husband's congressional office in Washington. She was the owner and operator of the radio-TV station KTBC in Austin, Texas, from 1942 to 1963, and the owner of several cattle ranches in Texas, as well as cotton and timberlands in Alabama. Lady Bird was an enthusiastic supporter of President Johnson's "war on poverty." Her other campaigns during her years as first lady include the Headstart Program and the "beautification" of Washington, D.C.

Mrs. Johnson was the recipient of many civil awards. Following her husband's presidency, she returned to Texas to write *White House Diary* (1970), and continue her efforts in beautification projects.

John Connally was a friend to both Lyndon and Lady Bird Johnson for over fifty years, and was an ally in both state and national political arenas.

Eulogy for John Connally by Lady Bird Johnson

Nellie, all the Connallys, President Nixon, and friends of John—it's been a wonderful life!

All the more wonderful because our family shared it with John and Nellie. We shared our youth, dreams, and ambitions. We shared campaigns and unending work. We shared births—deaths. We shared a war. There were times we even shared houses. There were laughter and good times. There was anguish.

John was always the young one. Always the strikingly handsome, magnetic, energetic can-do man—as Lyndon would say.

I remember once during the war, we were all at a cafe in Alabama and every person left his seat to peer out the window except Senator Wirtz, John, me, and our somewhat crusty middle-aged waitress. I asked the waitress what all the commotion was about. She said Clark Gable was stationed at Maxwell Field and everyone had gone to watch him walk down the street. She then turned to John and said, "You all don't have to go; you're just as handsome as he is!"

John walked in the room and you felt his presence, but not just because of how he looked. He knew how to make things happen. He knew this state and all of its 254 counties. He loved Texas. A whole generation of young folks reached majority with John Connally—the only governor they had known. Many subsequent generations have been educated at the expanded University (of Texas) system he masterfully led the fight for.

Some knew John as their governor, some their secretary of the navy, others their secretary of the treasury.

I knew him as our friend of half a century . . . the man I turned to to handle Lyndon's eulogy as he had so many other of the important moments of our lives.

He was a man I counted on and a man who was accountable always. Even in the roughest days, his character shone through.

When I think of John, his strength and vitality are intertwined with my image of Texas and that means a lot to me.

We bid him a loving farewell. Missing him with all our hearts, but rejoicing in his full and vigorous life.

Walt Disney

December 5, 1901 ~ December 15, 1966

Eulogy delivered by Roy O. Disney at a memorial service in Burbank, California

Walt Disney

The American artist and entrepreneur Walter Elias Disney was born in Chicago in 1906. During the early 1920s, he worked in animation with Ub Iwerks, and moved from Kansas City to Hollywood in 1923. His most famous creation, Mickey Mouse, appeared in the first cartoon with sound in 1928, with Disney himself providing Mickey his squeaky voice. He broke new ground in the 1930s with his colored cartoons, and in 1937 released the first feature-length animated film, *Snow White and the Seven Dwarfs*. These were followed by such other successes as *Pinocchio* (1940), *Dumbo* (1941), and *Bambi* (1942). *Fantasia,* released in 1940, was the first successful attempt to realize classical music in images.

By the 1950s, Disney had switched to nature films and those featuring live characters. He directed such swashbuckling films as *Robin Hood* (1952) and *Treasure Island* (1959). During this period he branched out into the growing television industry, producing such films as the *Davy Crockett* series, and the popular show, *The Mickey Mouse Club*.

Disney opened his first theme amusement park, Disneyland, in Anaheim, California, in 1955. This was followed in 1971 by the opening of the 27,000-acre Walt Disney World in Orlando, Florida. The entertainment empire he founded has spanned several generations—a continuing presence not only in American popular culture, but worldwide as well.

Roy O. Disney

Entertainment industry executive Roy O. Disney was born in Chicago in 1893, the son of Elias and Flora (Call) Disney and older brother of Walt Disney. He married Edna Francis in 1925, and had one son.

Roy Disney's business sense was the driving force behind his brother Walt's creative genius. In 1923, he lent Walt $250 to open a cartoon studio in Hollywood, eventually building the Disney empire into a giant in the world of business.

After Walt Disney's death, Roy Disney became the chairman of the board and chief executive officer, maintaining the vision created by his younger brother. He completed the creation of Walt Disney World in Orlando, Florida, concentrating his efforts on the financial success of the empire.

Roy Disney died on December 21, 1971, in Burbank, California.

Eulogy for Walt Disney by Roy O. Disney

The death of Walt Disney is a loss to all the people of the world. In everything he did, Walt had an intuitive way of reaching out and touching the hearts and minds of young and old alike. His entertainment was an international language. For more than forty years, people have looked to Walt Disney for the finest quality in family entertainment.

There is no way to replace Walt Disney. He was an extraordinary man. Perhaps there will never be another like him. I know that we who worked at his side for all these years will always cherish the years and the minutes we spent in helping Walt Disney entertain the people of the world. The world will always be a better place because Walt Disney was its master showman.

As president and chairman of the board of Walt Disney Productions, I want to assure the public, our stockholders, and each of our more than four thousand employees that we will continue to operate Walt Disney's company in the way that he established and guided it. Walt Disney spent his entire life, and almost every waking hour, in the creative planning of motion pictures, Disneyland, television shows, and all the other diversified activities that have carried his name through the years. Around him, Walt Disney gathered the kind of creative people who understood his way of communicating with the public through entertainment. Walt's ways were always unique, and he built a large organization, a team of creative people that he was justifiably proud of.

I think Walt would have wanted me to repeat his words to describe the organization he built over the years. Last October, when he accepted the "Showman of the World" award in New York, Walt said:

"The Disney organization now has more than four thousand employees. Many have been with us for over thirty years. They take great pride in the organization which they helped to build. Only through the talent, the labor, and the dedication of this staff could any Disney project get off the ground. We all think alike in the ultimate pattern."

Much of Walt Disney's energies had been directed to preparing for this day. It was Walt's wish that when the time came, he would have built an organization with the creative talents to carry on as he had established and directed it through the years. Today this organization has been built, and we will carry out this wish.

Walt Disney's preparation for the future is a solid, creative foundation. All of the plans for the future that Walt had begun—new motion pictures, the expansion of Disneyland, television production, and our Florida and Mineral King projects—will continue to move ahead. That is the way Walt wanted it to be.

Dwight D. Eisenhower

October 14, 1890 ~ March 28, 1969

Eulogy delivered by President Richard Nixon
at the funeral service in the Capitol Rotunda,
Washington, D.C., March 30, 1969

Dwight D. Eisenhower

American general and thirty-fourth president, Dwight David Eisenhower was born in Denison, Texas, the son of David Jacob and Elizabeth (Stover) Eisenhower. He graduated from the West Point Military Academy in 1915. During World War I, Eisenhower was assigned to military training camps, and earned a reputation as an organizer and trainer of men. After study at the Army War College, he served in the office of the assistant secretary for war (1929 to 1933). By 1933, he had become military assistant to General Douglas MacArthur, and accompanied him to the Philippines in 1935. With the outbreak of war in Europe in 1939, he obtained leave to return to duty in the United States.

Carefully groomed for the responsibility by General George C. Marshall, Eisenhower was sent to England as U.S. Commander in Europe in 1942. Following his successful conduct of the invasion of North Africa, he was selected as supreme commander for the 1944 invasion of France. After the war, he was appointed chief of staff of the U.S. Army (1945 to 1948).

From 1948 to 1950, he served as president of Columbia University, and in 1951 President Harry S Truman named him military commander of NATO. By 1952, the popularity he had gained in Europe swept him to nomination and ultimate victory in the presidential election. Standing as a Republican, he won by a large majority and was reelected in 1956. As president, Eisenhower's domestic achievements included civil rights acts in 1957 and 1960, and the establishment of the massive interstate highway system. In foreign affairs, he used a twofold approach—tough on communism and the preservation of peace. By the end of his second term, however, the Cold War had intensified.

In recent years his presidency has been subject to a favorable reassessment, now seen as maintaining stability during a difficult period.

After leaving office, Eisenhower retired to his farm in Gettysburg, Pennsylvania. He died in Washington, D.C., at the age of seventy-eight.

Richard Nixon

For a biographical sketch, see the eulogy for Richard Nixon, page 124. Nixon had served as vice president during both of Eisenhower's presidential terms. At the time of Eisenhower's death, Nixon was president himself.

Eulogy for Dwight D. Eisenhower by President Richard Nixon

Mrs. Eisenhower, Your Excellencies, friends of Dwight David Eisenhower in America and throughout the world:

We gather today in mourning, but also in gratitude.

We mourn Dwight Eisenhower's death, but we are grateful for his life.

We gather, also, conscious of the fact that in paying tribute to Dwight Eisenhower, we celebrate greatness. When we think of his place in history, we think, inevitably, of the other giants of those days of World War II and we think of the qualities of greatness and what his were that made him unique among all.

Once, perhaps without intending to do so, he, himself, put his finger on it. It was 1945, shortly after VE-Day, at a ceremony in London's historic Guildhall. The triumphant Supreme Commander of the Allied Forces in Europe was officially given the Freedom of the City of London.

In an eloquent address that day, Dwight Eisenhower said, "I come from the heart of America."

Perhaps no one sentence could better sum up what Dwight Eisenhower meant to a whole generation of Americans. He did come from the heart of America, not only from its geographical heart, but from its spiritual heart.

He exemplified what millions of parents hoped that their sons would be—strong, courageous, honest, and compassionate.

And with his own great qualities of heart, he personified the best in America.

It is, I think, a special tribute to Dwight Eisenhower that despite all of his honors, despite all of his great deeds, and his triumphs, we find ourselves today thinking first, not of his deeds but of his character. It was the character of the man, not what he did, but what he was that so captured the trust and faith and affection of his own people and of the people of the world.

Dwight Eisenhower touched something fundamental in America which only a man of immense force of mind and spirit could have brought so vibrantly alive. He was a product of America's soil and of its ideals, driven by a compulsion to do right and to do well; a man of deep faith who believed in God and trusted in His will; a man who truly loved his country and for whom the words "freedom" and "democracy" were not cliches, but they were living truths.

I know Mrs. Eisenhower would permit me to share with you the last words he spoke to her on the day he died. He said, "I have always loved my wife. I have always loved my children. I have always loved my grandchildren. And I have always loved my country." That was Dwight Eisenhower.

He was a man who gave enormously of himself. His way of relaxing from the intense pressures of office or command was to do something else intensely, whether as a fierce competitor on the golf course or executing one of those hauntingly beautiful paintings that he did with such meticulous care. But even more than this, he gave enormously of himself to people. People loved Dwight Eisenhower. But the other side of this coin was that he loved people.

He had the great leader's capacity to bring out the best in people. He had the great humanist's capacity to inspire people, to cheer them, to give them life.

I remember, for example, just a few months ago when I asked all of the members of the Cabinet to go out and call on him. Each of them returned with wonder and admiration and said, "You know, I went out there to cheer him up and instead I found he cheered me up."

His great love of people was rooted in his faith. He had a deep faith in the goodness of God and in the essential goodness of man as a creature of God.

This feeling toward people had another side. In the political world, strong passions are the norm and all too often these turn toward personal vindictiveness. People often disagreed with Dwight Eisenhower, but almost nobody ever hated him.

And this, I think, was because he, himself, was a man who did not know how to hate.

Oh, he could be aroused by a cause, but he could not hate a person. He could disagree strongly, even passionately, but never personally.

When people disagreed with him, he never thought of them as enemies. He simply thought, "Well, they don't agree with me."

I remember time after time, when critics of one sort or another were misrepresenting him or reviling him, he would sit back in his chair and with that wonderful half-smile and half-frown, he would say, "I am puzzled by those fellows." And he was genuinely puzzled by frenzy and by hate because he was incapable of it himself. He could never quite understand it in others.

The last time I saw him that was what he talked about. He was puzzled by the hatreds he had seen in our times. And he said the thing the world needs most today is understanding and an ability to see the other person's point of view and not to hate him because he disagrees.

That was Dwight Eisenhower.

And yet, of course, he was more than all of that. He had a side more evident to those of us who worked with him than to the rest of the world. He was a strong man. He was shrewd. He was decisive.

Time and again I have seen him make decisions that probably made the difference between war and peace for America and the world.

That was always when he was at his best. No matter how heated the arguments were, he was always then the coolest man in the room.

Dwight Eisenhower was that rarest of men—an authentic hero.

War brings the names of many men into the headlines and of those some few become national or even international heroes. But as the years then pass, their fame goes down.

But not so with Dwight Eisenhower. As the years passed, his stature grew: commander of the mightiest expeditionary force ever assembled; receiver of the surrender of the German armies in World War II; president of Columbia University; supreme commander of NATO; thirty-fourth president of the United States. The honors, the offices were there in abundance. Every trust that the American people had it in their power to bestow, he was given.

And, yet, he always retained a saving humility. His was the humility not of fear but of confidence. He walked with the great of the world, and he knew the greater human.

His was the humility of man before God and before the truth. His was the humility of a man too proud to be arrogant.

The pursuit of peace was uppermost in his mind when he ran for the presidency. And it was uppermost in his conduct of that office. And it is a tribute to his skill and determination that not since the 1930s has the nation enjoyed so long a period of peace, both at home and abroad, as the one that began in 1953 and continued through his presidency.

As commander of the mightiest allied force ever assembled, he was the right man at the right place at the right time.

And as president, once again he was the right man at the right place and at the right time.

He restored calm to a divided nation. He gave Americans a new measure of self-respect. He invested his office with dignity and respect and trust. He made Americans proud of their president, proud of their country, proud of themselves.

And if we in America were proud of Dwight Eisenhower, it was partly because he made us proud of America.

He came from the heart of America. And he gave expression to the heart of America and he touched the hearts of the world.

Many leaders are known and respected outside their own countries. Very few are loved outside their own countries. Dwight Eisenhower was one of those few. He was probably loved by more people in more parts of the world than any president America has ever had.

He captured the deepest feelings of free men everywhere. The principles he believed in, the ideals he stood for, these were bigger than his own country.

Perhaps he himself put it best again in that Guildhall speech in 1945. He said then, "Kinship among nations is not determined in such measurements as proximity, size and age. Rather, we should turn to those inner things, call them what you will, I mean those intangibles that are the real treasures that free men possess, to preserve his freedom of worship, his equality before the law, his liberty to speak and act as he sees fit, subject only to provisions that he not trespass upon similar rights of others.

"A Londoner will fight and so will a citizen of Abilene. When we consider these things, then the Valley of the Thames draws closer to the farms of Kansas and the plains of Texas."

Some men are considered great because they lead great armies or they lead powerful nations. For eight years now, Dwight Eisenhower has neither commanded an army nor led a nation. And, yet, he remained through his final days the world's most admired and respected man, truly the first citizen of the world.

As we marvel at this, it leads us once again to ponder the mysteries of greatness. Dwight Eisenhower's greatness derived not from his office, but from his character, from a unique moral force that transcended national boundaries, even as his own deep concern for humanity transcended national boundaries.

His life reminds us that there is a moral force in this world more powerful than the might of arms or the wealth of nations. This man who led the most powerful armies that the world has ever seen, this man who led the most powerful nation in the world, this essentially good and gentle and kind man, that moral force was his greatest.

For a quarter of a century, to the very end of his life, Dwight Eisenhower exercised a moral authority without parallel in America and in the world. And America and the world are better because of it.

And so today we render our final salute. It is a fond salute to a man we loved and cherished. It is a grateful salute to a man whose whole extraordinary life was consecrated to service. It is a profoundly respectful salute to a man larger than life who by any standard was one of the giants of our time.

Each of us here will have a special memory of Dwight Eisenhower.

I can see him now standing erect, straight, proud and tall, sixteen years ago as he took the oath of office as the thirty-fourth president of the United States of America.

We salute Dwight Eisenhower standing there in our memories, first in war, first in peace, and wherever freedom is cherished, first in the hearts of his fellow men.

Henry Fonda

May 16, 1905 ~ August 12, 1982

Tribute by Senator Max Baucus given in the Congress, August 16, 1982, and appearing as part of the *Congressional Record*

Henry Fonda

Actor Henry Fonda was born in Grand Island, Nebraska, the son of William Brace and Herberta (Jaynes) Fonda. He married Shirlee Adams and had three children. Fonda studied at the University of Minnesota from 1923 to 1925, and began acting with theater groups in Omaha and Des Moines. In 1928 he moved east, playing in small theaters in New England and New York City. After several years of supporting roles, he landed the lead in *The Farmer Takes a Wife* (1934), winning critical acclaim for his easy style.

Fonda went to Hollywood in 1935 to star in the film version of the play, and stayed to make several more films, including *Jezebel* (1938) and *Young Mr. Lincoln* (1939). During this period before the war, Fonda made two films for which he received resounding praise—*The Grapes of Wrath* (1940) and *The Ox Bow Incident* (1942). Fonda served in the United States Navy from 1942 to 1945, enlisting as seaman first class and eventually attaining the rank of lieutenant.

After the war, he continued to distinguish himself as an actor in such Westerns as *My Darling Clementine* (1946) and *Fort Apache* (1948). He returned to Broadway in 1948 as the title character and what many consider to be his finest role—*Mr. Roberts.* Fonda also starred in the 1955 film version, and continued to appear in films throughout the fifties and sixties, including *Twelve Angry Men* (1957) and *Advise and Consent* (1961).

In 1974, Fonda returned to Broadway in the one-man show *Clarence Darrow*. Loved for his ingenuous characters and straightforward manner, he was awarded a Tony in 1979 and a Kennedy Center for the Performing Arts Award in 1979. After appearing in over eighty films during a career that spanned four decades, Fonda was finally awarded an Academy Award for best actor for his role in *On Golden Pond* in 1991.

Max Baucus

Senator Max S. Baucus was born in Helena, Montana, on December 11, 1941, the son of John and Jean (Sheriff) Baucus. He married Wanda Minge in 1983. A graduate of Stanford University, he earned a B.A. in 1964 and an LL.B. in 1967. Baucus became a member of the bar in Washington, D.C., in 1969, and in Montana in 1972.

Baucus was staff attorney for the Civil Aeronautics Board, Washington, D.C., from 1967 to 1968, and in 1968 became a lawyer for the Securities and Exchange Commission (SEC). In 1970, he was appointed legal assistant to the chairman of the SEC, and returned to his private law practice in Missoula, Montana, in 1971.

Baucus was elected to the Montana House of Representatives in 1973 and in 1975 returned to Washington as Democratic representative for the First District of Montana. From 1975 to 1979, he was a member of the committee for appropriations. In 1979 he was elected senator from Montana. He has served as ranking senate minority member and on several committees, including environment and public works. Baucus has also been a member of the Senate Democratic steering and coordination committee.

Senator Baucus was a friend of Henry Fonda.

Tribute for Henry Fonda by Senator Max Baucus

Mr. President, a friend of mine and three generations of Americans died last week.

Most of us cannot remember a time when Henry Fonda was not entertaining and inspiring millions with his remarkable talent.

His exceptional acting ability, however, was by no means his most remarkable characteristic. Henry Fonda's integrity, honesty, and quiet courage in real life were his greatest attributes.

Many people believe that because he was such a natural and gifted actor, whose roles were often heroic, his fans just assumed he was that way in real life.

Those of us who knew Henry understood that it was the other way around. It was the honesty, thoughtfulness, and intelligence of Henry Fonda the man that was transferred into his acting. It was Henry Fonda the man that captured the hearts of Americans.

If there is ever to be an award for being fair and decent and honest and caring it will surely be called the Henry Fonda Award. And fortunately, because of the magic of film, Americans for a long, long time will have the opportunity and the privilege of knowing Henry Fonda, and this great man will continue to mold and influence American ideals. In life and in film, he was what we all want to be and what we all hope America is.

Henry Ford

July 30, 1863 ~ April 7, 1947

Tribute delivered by Edgar A. Guest on a national radio broadcast, April 9, 1947

Henry Ford

The American automobile engineer and manufacturer Henry Ford was born in Dearborn, Michigan, the son of Irish immigrants. Apprenticed to a machinist in Detroit at the age of fifteen, he began to experiment with a horseless carriage, and produced his first gasoline-driven motor car in 1896. During the next few years, while trying to get his car into production, he designed race cars, and was a successful racing driver. In 1903 he founded the Ford Motor Company.

Ford introduced the Model T in 1908, and pioneered the modern assembly line, which was producing cars by 1913. By 1928, fifteen million Model Ts were produced by these mass-production techniques.

A fervent pacifist, Ford was relatively uneducated, and thought "history is bunk." While he had significant mechanical abilities, his ideas were reached not by logic but by intuition. Ford tended to have unrealistic beliefs about the world, and in 1915 he tried to negotiate an end to the war by chartering a Peace Ship to Europe.

In 1919 he was succeeded by his son Edsel, but never completely relinquished control of the company. Refusing to recognize the decline of the Model T, the Ford Motor Company lost its first-place position to General Motors in the mid-1920s. While new innovations such as the V-8 engine in 1932 illustrated Henry Ford's mechanical genius, he stubbornly resisted the changes espoused by Edsel. Perhaps from the strain of struggling with his aging father, Edsel died at the age of fifty in 1943, and Henry once again took over the presidency.

In 1945, suffering the results of two strokes and unable to run the company any longer, Henry Ford finally turned control of the company over to Edsel's oldest son, Henry Ford II.

Edgar A. Guest

Writer Edgar Albert Guest was born in Birmingham, England, on August 20, 1881, the son of Edwin and Julia (Wayne) Guest. His family emigrated to the United States in 1891, and settled in Detroit, where he attended school. He married Nellie Crossman in 1906, and the couple had two children.

Guest first began working at the *Detroit Free Press* in 1895 as an office boy. He was moved up to a police reporter, and then an exchange editor, reading other newspapers and using their odds and ends, including verse, as fillers. Guest soon began inserting his own writing, and, after being discovered, was given his own column. He continued this work for over fifty years, and at the height of his career was syndicated in more than three hundred newspapers. His verse was sentimental in nature and spoke about the ups and downs of everyday life.

Guest also published over twenty collections of verse; his most popular was *A Heap o' Livin'* (1916), which went through more than thirty editions.

Edgar Guest died on August 5, 1959, and was buried in Detroit. He was a longtime friend of Henry Ford.

Tribute for Henry Ford by Edgar A. Guest

I would like to tell you about a truly great friend of mine and a benefactor of all mankind, known to presidents, potentates, princes, and the humble peoples of every land upon the earth, as Henry Ford.

Among those of us who knew him well he will walk no more, but so long as human achievements are cherished and remembered his name will be a living force and an inspiration to all the generations to follow.

Henry Ford has been called in the midst of his eighty-third year to join the great of the earth. Tonight he knows the answer to the mystery of life and death of which he often thought and talked. Life to him was a thrilling experience; a never-ending struggle for the perfection of the human soul. Among the few who have come closest to attaining that perfection in a single lifetime his name must be recorded.

We are all his debtors now. There is none of us, rich or poor, in humble or high place, whose life has not been bettered by his labor. He came into the world when the backs of men were weary and heavy-laden.

By the dreams he had, pursued and achieved, the burdens of drudgery were taken from the shoulders of the humble and given to steel and wheel.

He would not have us mourn for him too deeply. He knew that his loved ones and friends would be saddened by his absence, but, as he was often heard to say: "There is too much to do in a day to spend minutes of it in the futility of grief."

Once when he was asked by one who now and then walked the woods with him in springtime if he had not wished that his mother could have lived long enough to have seen and shared the glory of his triumphs, in the quiet and quaint way he had, he said softly: "I can think of no one who has gone whom I would recall."

Henry Ford had the gift of genius, but he had much more. Genius, though brilliant, can be bitter at times, harsh and selfish and disinterested in the lives of others. Henry Ford never showed those traits.

His was a sensitive heart and his was an understanding mind. He had known hardship and the pangs of disappointment; he had known the agony of wanting comforts for his loved ones which he could not supply. He had known what it means to be poor of purse, and he could and did read the eyes of the unhappy. He had both sympathy and pity for the woes of others.

It was out of that feeling for his fellows the five-dollar-a-day wage came when the daily universal rate of pay for a workman was a little less than two dollars. He called it good business to have as many contented men about him as were possible. It took courage of a rare sort to lead the way to a decent living wage for the common man.

Henry Ford woke early every morning eager to greet the day and all it held for him. Nothing was too small for him to notice. He loved the earth and all it grew and all that dwells upon it. He knew the birds by name and song and habits and found peace and happiness in their company.

He loved to escape and talk with humble men. He often said: "You can learn more from the thoughts of simple folk than you can from those of the learned and the wise. Wise minds know what can't be done, and they don't find out the things that can be done until someone not so wise comes along and tries them and does them."

Henry Ford will be missed. He will be missed in many places where kindness is still needed; he will be missed when it comes to right a wrong and to fight injustice is required; he will be missed by all the creatures of the woods and fields who found in him a friend; and he will be missed by many a struggling youth to whom a word of hope and encouragement would mean so much.

What an example he has set for boyhood to look up to and to follow! His life for generations to come will be a beacon light for all ambitious youths. I can hear his voice whispering down the years to young dreamers everywhere: "It can be done! Follow your light and learn by patient practice. Let neither sneer nor mockery daunt you. Believe in yourself; have faith in your ability and your purpose. Success will surely follow."

Not many come to earth so wise,
So tender and so true,
To show what faith and enterprise
And willing hands can do.
He proved how great a man can be
And gave so much to us.
Now, Lord, we give him back to Thee,
A soul victorious.

Robert Frost

March 26, 1874 ~ January 29, 1963

Tribute delivered by President John F. Kennedy,
Amherst College, Massachusetts, October 27, 1963

Robert Frost

One of America's leading poets of the twentieth century, Robert Lee Frost was born in San Francisco. The family moved to Massachusetts after his father's death in 1885. Although he studied at Harvard (1897 to 1899), he did not graduate, and spent the next ten years as a teacher and New Hampshire farmer. He wrote during these years, but the poems were rarely published.

In 1912, Frost sold the farm and used the proceeds to move his family to England, where he devoted himself to writing. In 1913 *A Boy's Will* was published in London, followed by *North of Boston* in 1914. Both books were subsequently published in America, bringing Frost an international reputation. During his stay in England, he was greatly influenced by such Georgian poets as Rupert Brooke, finding their pastoral subjects and style similar to his own.

Frost returned to the United States in 1915, and with the success of his two books bought another farm in New Hampshire, where he continued to write. While his poetry is often associated with the people and landscapes of New England, the dimensions of its philosophy are universal.

Frost was the recipient of innumerable honors from academic, literary, and public institutions. His powerful, beautiful lyrics were awarded the Pulitzer Prize for poetry four times: *New Hampshire* (1923), *Collected Poems* (1930), *A Further Range* (1936), and *A Witness Tree* (1942). He was professor of poetry at Harvard from 1939 to 1943 before returning to Amherst, where he taught from 1949 to 1963.

John F. Kennedy

For a biographical sketch, see the tribute for John F. Kennedy, page 67.
President Kennedy was a friend and admirer of Robert Frost.

Tribute for Robert Frost by President John F. Kennedy

This day, devoted to the memory of Robert Frost, offers an opportunity for reflection which is prized by politicians as well as by others and even by poets. For Robert Frost was one of the granite figures of our time in America. He was supremely two things—an artist and an American.

A nation reveals itself not only by the men it produces but also by the men it honors, the men it remembers.

In America our heroes have customarily run to men of large accomplishments. But today this college and country honors a man whose contribution was not to our size but to our spirit; not to our political beliefs but to our insight; not to our self-esteem but to our self-comprehension.

In honoring Robert Frost, we therefore can pay honor to the deepest sources of our natural strength. That strength takes many forms, and the most obvious forms are not always the most significant.

The men who create power make an indispensable contribution to the nation's greatness. But the men who question power make a contribution just as indispensable, especially when that questioning is disinterested.

For they determine whether we use power or power uses us. Our national strength matters, but the spirit which informs and controls our strength matters just as much. This was the special significance of Robert Frost.

He brought an unsparing instinct for reality to bear on the platitudes and pieties of society. His sense of the human tragedy fortified him against self-deception and easy consolation.

"I have been," he wrote, "one acquainted with the night."

And because he knew the midnight as well as the high noon, because he understood the ordeal as well as the triumph of the human spirit, he gave his age strength with which to overcome despair.

At bottom he held a deep faith in the spirit of man. And it's hardly an accident that Robert Frost coupled poetry and power. For he saw poetry as the means of saving power from itself.

When power leads man toward arrogance, poetry reminds him of his limitations. When power narrows the areas of man's concern, poetry reminds him of the richness and diversity of his existence. When power corrupts, poetry cleanses.

For art establishes the basic human truths which must serve as the touchstones of our judgment. The artist, however faithful to his personal vision of reality, becomes the last champion of the individual mind and sensibility against an intrusive society and an officious state.

The great artist is thus a solitary figure. He has, as Frost said, "a lover's quarrel with the world." In pursuing his perceptions of reality, he must often sail against the currents of his time. This is not a popular role.

If Robert Frost was much honored during his lifetime, it was because a good many preferred to ignore his darker truths.

Yet in retrospect we see how the artist's fidelity has strengthened the fiber of our national life. If sometimes our great artists have been the most critical of our society, it is because their sensitivity and their concern for justice, which must motivate any true artist, makes them aware that our nation falls short of its highest potential.

I see little of more importance to the future of our country and our civilization than full recognition of the place of the artist. If art is to nourish the roots of our culture, society must set the artist free to follow his vision wherever it takes him.

We must never forget that art is not a form of propaganda; it is a form of truth. And as Mr. MacLeish once remarked of poets, "There is nothing worse for our trade than to be in style."

In free society, art is not a weapon and it does not belong to the sphere of polemics and ideology. Artists are not engineers of the soul.

It may be different elsewhere. But democratic society—in it—the highest duty of the writer, the composer, the artist is to remain true to himself and to let the chips fall where they may.

In serving his vision of the truth, the artist best serves his nation. And the nation which disdains the mission of art invites the fate of Robert Frost's hired man—"the fate of having nothing to look backward to with pride and nothing to look forward to with hope."

I look forward to a great future for America—a future in which our country will match its military strength with our moral restraint, its wealth with our wisdom, its power with our purpose.

I took forward to an America which will not be afraid of grace and beauty, which will protect the beauty of our national environment, which will preserve the great old American houses and squares and parks of our national past, and which will build handsome and balanced cities for our future.

I look forward to an America which will reward achievement in the arts as we reward achievement in business or statecraft.

I look forward to an America which will steadily raise the standards of artistic accomplishment and which will steadily enlarge cultural opportunities to all of our citizens.

And I look forward to an America which commands respect throughout the world not only for its strength but for its civilization as well.

And I look forward to a world which will be safe not only for democracy and diversity but also for personal distinction.

Robert Frost was often skeptical about projects for human improvement. Yet I do not think he would disdain this hope.

As he wrote during the uncertain days of the Second World War:

> Take human nature altogether since time began . . .
> And it must be a little more in favor of man,
> Say a fraction of one percent at the very least . . .
> Our hold on the planet wouldn't have so increased.

Because of Mr. Frost's life and work, because of the life and work of this college, our hold on this planet has increased.

Pancho Gonzales

May 9, 1928 ~ July 3, 1995

Tribute by Bud Collins, *Washington Post*, July 5, 1995

Pancho Gonzales

American tennis player Richard A. ("Pancho") Gonzales was born in Los Angeles, the son of Manuel A. and Carmen (Alire) Gonzales. His first marriage, which ended in divorce, produced five children. In 1972 he married for a second time and fathered one daughter. Gonzales's third marriage was to Rita Agassi in 1984.

A natural athlete who was never professionally coached or trained, Gonzales was a powerful player and fierce competitor. He won his first U.S. Open singles championship in 1948, and successfully defended his title the following year. In 1949 he won championships for grass and clay, as well as the U.S. Indoor title.

Turning professional, Gonzales dominated the tennis circuit throughout the 1950s, retiring from the pro tour in 1963. In 1969, competing at Wimbledon against Charlie Pasarell, he won the longest match in the competition's history—five hours and twenty-two minutes. The following year, at age forty-two, Gonzales defeated then top-ranked Rod Laver in two matches.

In later years, many of Gonzales's peers observed that had he not turned professional at such an early age, he could have won at least one Wimbledon singles title during the peak of his prowess. Gonzales died in Las Vegas, Nevada, at age sixty-seven.

Bud Collins

Bud Collins was born in Berea, Ohio, and attended Baldwin-Wallace College in Berea, where he earned a bachelor of arts degree in 1951.

Collins began covering tennis in 1955 for the *Boston Herald* and later became a permanent staff writer. In 1964, he moved to the *Boston Globe,* and for more than thirty years has been a general sports and travel columnist for that paper. He made his television commentary debut in

1963, when he covered the U.S. Indoor National Doubles Championships for a Boston television station, and has covered virtually every major tennis event on the professional circuit since then.

Collins joined NBC Sports in 1964, assigned to cover the U.S. National Tennis Championships from Forest Hills, New York. He also covered the World Championship Tennis (WCT) Tournaments in 1972. Since then, Collins has provided commentary for all of NBC's tennis telecasts, and has covered twenty-four consecutive Wimbledon championships for the network.

Collins is known as both a pioneer and "guru" in the world of tennis broadcasting. On July 9, 1994, he was inducted into the International Tennis Hall of Fame. An established tennis player, Collins won the U.S. Indoor Mixed Doubles Championship with partner Janet Hopps in 1961. He is the author of four books, including *Bud Collins' Modern Encyclopedia of Tennis,* published in 1994.

Collins was a friend of Pancho Gonzales and covered him throughout his career.

Tribute for Pancho Gonzales by Bud Collins

Wimbledon patrons, an orderly crowd, seldom hiss and boo, but they gave Pancho Gonzales the vocal business that dank June evening twenty-six years ago. He was forty-one years old and the Old Wolf was starting to look it, silver highlights in the sumptuous jet mane, especially as he trudged sourly from Centre Court in a hailstorm of negative noise.

The problem was he had pouted and aimlessly pottered through the 6–1 second set against Charlie Pasarell, muttering that it was too dark to play. He had screamed that sentiment at the imperious referee, Captain Mike Gibson, after losing the opening set, 24–22. "Play on, Mr. Gonzales!" ordered Gibson from behind his guardsman's mustache. Pancho complied, half-heartedly, reaping consumer disapproval when the referee did close proceedings.

Gonzales was two sets behind in the first round, and giving away fifteen years to Pasarell, the No. 5 American. He fumed most of the night, playing cards with his wife until dawn while winding down. Hours later, back on Centre Court, Gonzales was rejuvenated. Once again the ageless, peerless competitor, the predatory wolf, he created one of the game's masterpieces, and left the full-house gathering of fifteen thousand—and Pasarell—raving and gasping.

Crashing out seven match points in the fifth set (twice from 0–40),

Gonzales turned the jeers of the previous dusk to hosannas as he beat Pasarell, 22–24, 1–6, 16–14, 6–3, 11–9.

Conversations turned to that dinger today as word that Gonzales died of cancer Monday night at sixty-seven in Las Vegas reached the Big W, the tournament he didn't win only because of the segregated conditions of tennis during his best days. Then, traditional tournaments were limited to alleged amateurs. After winning the U.S. Open in 1949, Gonzales sought his fortune with the outlaws, the out-and-out pros, and didn't make it back to Wimbledon for nearly two decades, until open competition dawned in 1968. He was forty, yet a factor, a quarterfinalist at the French and U.S. opens.

Ted Schroeder, loser of the 1949 Open final to Gonzales, said, "You could never be too far ahead of Pancho. I led him by two sets in '49 so I know how Pasarell felt here in '69."

A two-part comeback of comebacks, it consumed five hours twelve minutes, a jewel from the time before tie-breakers and therapeutic furniture. No chairs were there to sag on at changeovers. You just kept moving and playing.

Richard Alonso "Pancho" Gonzales—Richard to his friends, "Gorgo" to his few colleagues on the lonely pro tour of one-night stands—kept moving so long at the top level that he was still dangerous into his forty-fourth year, a fiery patriarch. Nobody ever played tennis better. But the fire has burned out. This king is dead, and his like won't reappear.

Schroeder said, "He came from the wrong side of the tracks, a Chicano in L.A., but he carried himself as proudly as a Spanish nobleman." He had pride in performance, a ruggedly handsome man with a scarred cheek and soft voice.

Nobody called the volcanic Pancho "Gorgo" to his face. It stood for Gorgonzola—the big cheese—and for years he was just that, carrying the fragile pro game around the world in his satchel. Pancho and pro tennis were synonymous.

"He's not the best player anymore." That was a slightly aggrieved Rod Laver in 1964, when Laver was, and deprived Gonzales a ninth U.S. Pro title in a splendid rainstormed final in Longwood, Massachusetts. "But nobody—including Pancho—knows that. He's the one player everyone knows and wants to see."

Seeing Gonzales at his greatest might have involved squeezing into a small armory or a high school gym when the pro caravan hit town, pitching its portable canvas court on whatever flooring, including ice. It was a king-of-the-hill tour. Gonzales against the latest hotshot Wimbledon or U.S. champ lured to professionalism by promoter Jack Kramer's dollars. Frank Sedgman, Tony Trabert, Ken Rosewall, Lew Hoad, Ashley Cooper, Pancho Segura, Alex Olmedo—a Hall of Fame parade—all tried to knock him off his green canvas hill. But Pancho won and stayed king, singing the magnificent serve, moving so fluidly, confronting the foe as though, said his closest pal, Segura, "he didn't want to do any more than kill you."

"It was a night-after-night nightmare," Rosewall said, shaking his head. "An experience that doesn't exist now. Imagine playing Sampras or Agassi almost every night throughout a year." Rosewall, a callow twenty-two, did very well, but he lost like everybody else.

"Remember that cold winter night at Boston Garden?" It was 1957, and Gonzales was conducting a three-way battle: against persistent Rosewall, also a more persistent courtside heckler and the insistent press with their insidious typewriters. In his rage to play and win, Gonzales let no one interfere.

Pausing in his decisive 19–17 set win to silence the loud critic in the first row, Gonzales intended to put his service grip on the poor guy's windpipe. At that moment the man in the next seat stood up to his full, muscular, six feet seven saying, "Why don't you just play, Pancho?" It was Jungle Jim Loscutoff, the Boston Celtics' enforcer.

Though six feet two, a magnificent athlete, Gonzales could see the wisdom in returning to quelling Rosewall and the clacking reporters in their balcony nest. Becoming an ack-ack gun, he sprayed the journalists with a barrage of balls. That turned off the labors of the survivors. Then he finished Rosewall.

"We didn't make much money but we had a lot of fun," said Segura. "But if you beat him, he might not talk to you for days. But he had a big heart. Difficult guy but honorable."

Gonzales once recalled his rookie pro campaign: "Two guys were the show, and the show went on. That tour, '49–'50, I got beat by Jack Kramer, who was also my boss. The promoter. I showed up one night, could hardly walk with a bum ankle, and told Jack I couldn't play. He says to me, 'Kid, we always play,' and got a doctor to shoot up the ankle with novocaine. That's the way it was."

The tennis show goes on, but without a majestic ornament who showed a couple of generations the wonder of power, presence, and passion within his rectangle.

Helen Hayes

October 10, 1900 ~ March 17, 1993

Eulogy delivered by Cliff Robertson

Helen Hayes

The "queen mother" of the American stage, Helen Hayes was born Helen Brown in Washington, the daughter of Francis Van Arnum and Catherine Estell (Hayes) Brown. In 1928, she married playwright Charles MacArthur; the couple had one child, James.

Hayes first appeared on stage at age six, and made her first appearance on Broadway in 1909. She landed her first starring role in 1920 as a flapper in *Bab, the Sub-Deb,* and continued in light comedy through the 1920s.

Her first critical acclaim was for her portrayal of the tragic heroine in *Coquette* (1927), and she was a box-office sensation in *Mary of Scotland* (1933 to 1934). Her role as Queen Victoria in *Victoria Regina* (1937 to 1938) was said to have been one of her personal favorites. Subsequent theatrical successes include *Harriet* (1943 to 1945) and *Happy Birthday* (1946), for which she won the first of her three Tony awards. During the fifties she appeared in *The Wisteria Trees* (1950), *Mrs. McThing* (1952), and *Time Remembered* (1957), for which she was awarded her second Tony. She retired from the stage in 1972.

Hayes's first major film was in 1931, *The Sin of Madelon Claudet,* for which she won an Academy Award in 1932. Her other films include *A Farewell to Arms* (1932) and *Anastasia* (1956), in which she endeared herself to many as the Dowager Empress. Hayes was awarded an Oscar for best supporting actress for her role as the elderly stowaway in *Airport* (1970).

Hayes appeared on television in the series *The Snoop Sisters,* which ran from 1972 to 1974, and played Miss Marple in the movie *Murder with Mirrors* in 1985. She was also the author of several books, including two novels, *Our Best Years* (1986) and *Where the Truth Lies* (1988), as well as an autobiography, *My Life in Three Acts* (1990).

During her long and distinguished career, Hayes was the supporter of many causes and the recipient of countless awards. She served as president of the American National Theatre and Academy, and second vice president of the Actors Fund from 1975 to 1993. She received medals from the city of New York and the Freedoms Foundation, and was presented a presidential Medal of Freedom as well as a National Medal of Arts. She made her home in Nyack, New York, for many years, and died there at the age of ninety-two.

Cliff Robertson

Actor, writer, and director Cliff Robertson was born in La Jolla, California, on September 9, 1925, the son of Clifford Parker and Audrey (Willingham) Robertson. In 1966 he married Dina Merrill. The couple had two daughters and were later divorced.

Robertson's films include *Picnic* (1956), *PT 109* (1963), *The Best Man* (1964), and *Charley* (1968), for which he won the 1969 Academy Award for best actor. His later movies were *3 Days of the Condor* (1975), *The Sunset Boys* (1995), and *Escape from L.A.* in 1996.

Robertson was also a familiar face on television, appearing in several made-for-TV movies and miniseries, including the Emmy award–winning *The Game* (1968) and *A Tree Grows in Brooklyn.*

A member of the Screen Actors Guild, Robertson has been a member of its New York chapter's board of directors since 1980. He is also a member of the Directors Guild and the Writers Guild, as well as the New York–based Players Club. He was the winner of the Theatre World award in 1970, and in 1985 he was granted the *Advertising Age* award.

Eulogy for Helen Hayes by Cliff Robertson

I first met Miss Hayes on the radio. She was in front of a microphone. I was in front of a Philco. Close—very close. The volume was low—my excitement high. It was late for eight year olds and the Philco had been turned off with the lights. But turned back on with the dark.

The Philco was more than a co-conspirator with the eight year old in that sleepy California town—it was his closest friend. It opened windows to the world—let voices come into the theatre of his mind. The curtain came up as the amber dial found the station. The station where the lady spoke. The lady with that voice. That unmistakable voice. That voice that quickened his pulse and lifted him to another world. A world where the lady reigned supreme.

I was but one of her hypnotized subjects. She was my queen then; she is my queen now. She was my very first lady of my theatre. And always will be.

Carl Hubbell

June 22, 1903 ~ November 21, 1988

Eulogy delivered by Vernon Markwell at the memorial service, Meeker, Oklahoma, High School, November 28, 1988

Carl Hubbell

American baseball great Carl Owen Hubbell grew up in Meeker, Oklahoma. He began his baseball career with the Detroit Tigers' farm team in the 1920s, throwing what Ty Cobb referred to as "that thing"—a screwball. The pitch eventually twisted his left arm to the point where the palm of his hand faced out. Hubbell reached the majors in 1928, signing with the New York Giants at age twenty-five.

In 1929, Hubbell pitched a no-hitter against Pittsburgh, and in 1933 played what he considered to be his greatest game, the famous eighteen-inning, 1-to-0 shutout over the Cardinals. Hubbell played seven All-Star games. On July 10, 1934, in his second All-Star appearance, Hubbell faced the power hitters of the American League: Babe Ruth, Lou Gehrig, Jimmie Foxx, Al Simmons, and Joe Cronin. He struck out all five with only twenty-three pitches.

Hubbell was named the National League's Most Valuable Player in 1933 and 1936, and was elected to the National Baseball Hall of Fame at Cooperstown, New York, in 1947. During his career, Hubbell won 253 games, pitched 3,589 innings, and recorded 1,678 strikeouts. Hubbell retired as a field director of the New York Giants farm system in 1977 and moved to Mesa, Arizona.

Vernon Markwell

Vernon Markwell was born January 21, 1932, on a small farm in Meeker, Oklahoma, to Harve and Zeffie Markwell, the last of five children. Living all his life in Meeker, he married Gail Lewis in 1951, and the couple have three children and six grandchildren. An auctioneer and real estate broker, Markwell has owned his business, Markwell Auction and Real Estate, for thirty-five years. It is a family operation serving the entire state of Oklahoma. Active in community service, he has served as president of several organizations, including the Jaycees, Lions Club, and the Meeker Chamber of Commerce.

Mr. Markwell was a close friend of Carl Hubbell.

Eulogy for Carl Hubbell by Vernon Markwell

We are all assembled here today for one reason—to remember Carl Hubbell, the baseball great . . . and the man.

As I look out over this host of people gathered here today, family, friends, admirers, colleagues, I think how appropriate it is for a man to return home for his final resting place.

Carl's story began in those first years after the Hubbell family had moved to Meeker, living in a rented cotton farm as did so many people in those years. It was here on the farm that Carl began to throw rocks and a worn out baseball at a mark on the side of the barn, learning that he had a real talent to throw a baseball. In high school, he played with some other talented young men, the Waner boys, who too became Hall of Famers. When he graduated from high school, he went to work for an oil company. That same year, he was signed by Cushing in the Oklahoma State League. The next year, Carl pitched briefly with Ardmore and Oklahoma City.

By 1925, when he won seventeen and lost thirteen in the Western League, Carl, a twenty-two-year-old left hander, had already begun to throw the screwball, which he had developed when seeking to turn the ball over to make it sink.

He was then sold to Detroit.

He did not become discouraged when the Detroit Tigers told him he had better give up that screwball and learn to pitch straight. Ty Cobb was the Tiger's player/manager at that time.

After being sent to Beaumont, Texas, it was there that the Giants' scout saw him pitch and called New York. As he began his career with the Giants, it was reported that Carl respected McGraw of the Giants because Carl was young and made some mistakes and McGraw was understanding.

Carl achieved greatness as a "Major League Left-Handed Screwball Pitcher"; and his ability to effectively control the pitching of the baseball led him to remarkable accomplishments, the winning of games, the setting of records, the receiving of awards, national recognition . . . yeah, . . . even international fame.

But you see—Carl did not always have that complete control of the baseball.

And that brings us to a very important part of remembering Carl Hubbell and what he was really like.

Carl, I believe, had many great characteristics, and one of the greatest was the determination to be the very best that he could be in what he did. Although Carl, no doubt, had difficult times in those early years of baseball, he did not become discouraged in the mid-twenties, moving from club to club, before he reached the Majors and signed with the New York Giants in 1928 at the age of twenty-five.

He wasn't satisfied with just being average, using only a part of his talent or ability, but rather . . . he continued to work hard toward being the very best that he could be.

It has been written that on July 10, 1934, "a golden moment in baseball history was recorded" at that second All-Star game, when Carl faced those power hitters of the American League. He was able to strike out all five of them, one by one, with only twenty-three pitches, beginning with Babe Ruth, then Lou Gehrig, then Jimmie Foxx, then Al Simons, and finally Joe Cronin, and he did so because he was striving to become the very best that he could be.

You see, Carl had then reached the point where he could set up the hitters with the fast ball, and the curve ball, then use the screwball to strike them out.

Carl was selected to play in the All-Star games seven times, and his legendary strikeout feat in that 1934 game is unquestionably the outstanding pitching performance in the All-Stars' fifty-five-year history.

However, there were other unforgettable Carl Hubbell games: A no-hitter against Pittsburgh on May 8, 1929; the famous eighteen-inning, 1-to-10 shutout win over the Cardinals on July 2, 1933, with Carl pitching perfect ball in twelve innings, striking out twelve batters and allowing no walks; and a ten-inning, 2-to-0 win over the Boston Braves in 1933 in which Carl not only did not allow a walk, but did not even have a three-and-two count to a single batter. He also had a one-hitter against Brooklyn in 1940 when he faced only the minimum of twenty-seven hitters.

Carl's contribution to the Giants' efforts in the 1930s, when they won three pennants, cannot be described adequately by merely reciting his record. He was the ultimate stopper, consistently winning important games as a starting pitcher and saving games in relief. In recognition, Carl was named the National League's Most Valuable Player in 1933 and 1936. Other outstanding accomplishments include a twenty-four consecutive game winning streak, the last sixteen games in 1936 and his first eight games in 1937; his string of five successive twenty-game winning seasons; and forty-six and a third consecutive scoreless innings pitched. Carl won two of the Giants' four 1933 World Series games against the Senators with an unbelievable 0.00 earn run average and fifteen strikeouts in twenty innings. All in all, Carl won 253 games, pitched 3,589 innings, and recorded 1,678 strikeouts in his career.

On one occasion when talking with Carl about what he considered some of his best accomplishments, of course he mentioned the 1934 All-Star game, but he also seemed pleased with the eighteen-inning shutout game, and the twenty-four-consecutive-games winning streak.

For all of these and other great accomplishments, he was recognized and elected to the National Baseball Hall of Fame at Cooperstown, New York, in 1947.

And that brings us to remember some of the other great characteristics of Carl Hubbell . . . for through all of these years and all of these outstanding achievements, even to becoming famous, Carl was and remained a humble man, a kind man, a modest man, and a quiet man.

For instance, when the subject of errors on the playing field behind him was brought up, Carl was quoted as saying, "Nobody makes an error on purpose. All you can do is bear down harder and resist the temptation to blame the other fellow."

Many times, he was described as sensational, a fine man, and a man who thinks.

Through all of the many interviews over the years, Carl always seemed to praise other ballplayers and never put himself on a higher level. It is quoted that "Carl was a humble sort who talked about himself only after every other subject was exhausted." I learned only a few days ago that Carl had appeared in a movie in the early fifties. He never mentioned this movie unless someone asked him. He was in a movie with Edward G. Robinson, and this was the type of thing that many would have bragged about, but you would have to have known about it and to have asked Carl for him to have talked about it.

Carl was a team player. Fellow pitching great Waite Hoyt once said, "Hubbell is a great pitcher; his influence on the ball club is great; his emotions, if he has any, never affect him."

Fellow Hall-of-Famer Jocko Conlan, a retired umpire, recently said, "Carl wasn't argumentative. He wasn't a very talkative person, but he was a wonderful fella. He never caused a fuss when I was officiating a game."

Of course, Carl was a competitor and may have felt it necessary, once in a while, to walk back of the pitching mound and look out into center field just to let the umpire know he didn't exactly agree with the last call. But, as Conlan said, "His emotions never affected him."

In 1977, when Carl retired from playing and from working as a field director of the New York Giants farm system, he moved to Mesa, Arizona.

I remember in 1978 the town of Meeker was seventy-five years old and we were planning a big celebration sponsored by the Chamber of Commerce. Some of us were determined to get Carl Hubbell to come and be our guest of honor. (It just happened Carl was going to be seventy-five years old that summer, too.)

We began to call him, inviting him to come and share this date in time with us . . . and he came.

Everyone was so glad to see him and he was glad to see everyone here. Young and old . . . and all in between, wanted to shake his hand, talk to him, take his picture, maybe even get an autograph, hopefully on a baseball. The new baseball field here at the high school was also dedicated the "Carl Hubbell Field" at that time. This was the beginning of a renewed friendship with Carl and his hometown.

During that visit, Carl came to me and said he had decided to donate his memorabilia to the town of Meeker, if a suitable place could be found for it. I assured him that we would provide a suitable place. I could tell he really wanted his baseball things here. It came as a wonderful surprise to this town when he made that announcement at the celebration before seven thousand people. Once again, showing generosity to his hometown.

In 1980, I remember Carl coming to my office and talking with me about his baseball keepsakes. I saw then another great characteristic of Carl. He talked with me about the museum and how he always wanted it to be free for everyone to visit, especially the young, for he thought that if they were able to see how he, from a very simple beginning as a farm boy from central Oklahoma, could accomplish the things that he did . . . maybe, just maybe, they could be inspired to a life of dedication and determination to reaching their goals in life. I saw once again this attitude of determination, humbleness, plus concern for others. Carl possessed such fine qualities.

In recent years, Carl has been honored nationally, by other states, and twice by his home state, Oklahoma. In 1984, Carl was honored by the Oklahoma Sports Headliner Awards banquet along with several other Oklahomans, one of which was Wyman Tisdale. On June 8, 1986, Carl was the first inductee into the Oklahoma Sports Hall of Fame. The painting of Carl by Tommy McDonald, who used to play football with the

Sooners, now hangs in the museum. Due to Carl's health, he was unable to attend either of these events, but was proud of these two awards.

After a ten-year friendship with Carl and as caretaker of his baseball keepsakes, as a member of the board of directors of the Carl Hubbell Museum, many times Carl has called me about something he wanted to talk about, or sent some item or letter he had received that he wanted to put into the museum. Gail, my wife, and I were amazed at the persons who contacted him these last years. Doctors, judges, other state officials, fellow baseball players, baseball managers, sportswriters, and many of his fans. He loved baseball; he loved the museum and was proud of it. Carl was a happy, contented man. He described his contentment in an article this way:

"I've now had some kind of association with baseball for almost sixty-one years. Everything that's come to me has equaled or exceeded my hopes. How many men of my limited education have been so lucky? I'd love to do it all over again and have it turn out exactly as it is today."

Over the last eleven years, Carl became friends with a gentleman by the name of Ken Brown. Mr. Brown described Carl as a happy man, happy he had a chance to pitch. He described him further as never wanting much more than that.

Although Carl was somewhat hindered by his strokes, he did not just give up. His last few years were spent enjoying his friends, going to the Cactus League games with them, going to the bowling alley, and going to the park to watch the guys play horseshoes.

Carl maintained a humorous side. I remember when the Carl Hubbell Museum was opened, a question was asked of Carl, "What do you attribute your baseball achievements to?" Carl did not crack a smile, but turned to the person who addressed the question and slowly said,"Hunger!" Then, he laughed.

He also was a man that could take some kidding. At the same time, he was joined by Joe Moore, a former Giant teammate. They were talking to the crowd that had gathered at the museum about the eighteen-inning 1-to-0 shutout in July, 1939 against the Cardinals. We had surprised Carl by having Joe Moore there that day and Joe was the player who scored the one run in the bottom of the eighteenth. Someone asked about the run that won the game. Jo Jo Moore grinned and looked at Carl and said, "Shoot, I knew Carl was about to run out of stuff after eighteen innings, so I decided to come home and score the run to end the game." Carl enjoyed that story as well as the crowd.

Carl's good qualities and characteristics are summed up in one paragraph in a letter sent to him in 1982 from a fan.

Now let's get the setting for this—

This man was only twelve years old when Carl pitched to fame in that 1934 All-Star game. The man wrote about how he and his brother listened to that game on a radio in a 1932 Chevy, and how he had always waited for the paper to come to read about Carl Hubbell, the famous left-handed screwball pitcher. And now fifty years later, being a retired postal employee, and now over sixty years old, this man from Virginia wrote:

"Thanks, Carl Hubbell, for being such a big part of my life, although you had no choice in the happening. Thanks for the beautiful career you had, for the marvelous ability you displayed through the years, both as a player and a gentleman; looking back on it all must make you a very proud man. Be sure that your pitching for the Giants made this fellow a mighty happy youngster for many a year. I'm just glad that you have been such a big part of my life."

Eight years ago when Carl and I talked about this day, this very day, when he asked me to do this favor for him, I learned about another great quality Carl had, and a quality every man should have. He said to me, "Vernon, I just want to be a friend to everyone, and everyone be a friend to me."

He was called "The Meal Ticket," "Hub," "King Carl," "The Magnificent," "The Meeker Magician" . . . and . . . he was called a friend to many, many, many people. He was my friend . . . and your friend.

I think of part of an old favorite hymn of mine that makes me think of Carl, and maybe it will make you think of him, too. It is entitled:

As the Life of a Flower

As the Life of a Flower
As a breath or a sigh
So the years that we live
As a dream hasten by.

True, today we are here,
But tomorrow may see
Just a grave in the vale
And a memory of me.

As the Life of a Flower
Be our lives pure and sweet;
May we brighten the way
For the friends that we greet.

And sweet incense arise
From our hearts as we live
Close to Him who doth teach
Us to love and forgive.

As the Life of a Flower
As a breath or a sigh
So the years glide away
And alas we must die.

Jacob Javits

May 18, 1904 ~ March 7, 1986

Eulogy delivered by Senator Daniel P. Moynihan,
New York City, March 1986

Jacob Javits

United States senator and lawyer Jacob K. Javits was born in New York City, the son of Morris and Ida (Littman) Javits. He married Marian Ann Borris in 1947, and the couple had three children. Javits received a bachelor's of law degree from New York University in 1926, and over his lifetime was the recipient of thirty-seven honorary degrees.

Javits entered into private practice in New York City in 1927 and joined the U.S. Army in 1942. A major, he served as assistant to chief of operations, serving in both the European and Pacific theaters of operations from 1942 to 1945. He was discharged as a colonel, and decorated with the Legion of Merit.

Javits was elected to the U.S. House of Representatives in 1947, where he served the Twenty-First New York District until 1954. He was New York state's attorney general from 1954 to 1957. Javits returned to Washington in 1957 as a senator from New York, where he remained until 1981. A liberal Republican who initially was a supporter of the war in Vietnam, Javits introduced legislation that became the War Powers Act (1973), restricting the president's authority to commit troops abroad.

After leaving the Senate, Javits was assistant professor of public affairs at Columbia University. A prolific author, his books include *Discrimination U.S.A.* (1960), *Who Makes War* (1973), and *Javits, The Autobiography of a Public Man* (1981). Javits was awarded the Presidential Medal of Freedom in 1983, and was a member of the American Legion, Veterans of Foreign Wars, and numerous other civic organizations. He was a lifelong resident of New York City.

Daniel P. Moynihan

Senator and educator Daniel Patrick Moynihan was born in Tulsa, Oklahoma, on March 16, 1927, the son of John Henry and Margaret Ann

(Phipps) Moynihan. He married Elizabeth Therese Brennan in 1955, and the couple have three children. He graduated from Tufts in 1948; in 1949 he received his master's from the Fletcher School of Law and Diplomacy, and he was granted a Ph.D. in 1961 from the same institution. Fletcher later awarded him an honorary LL.D. in 1968. Moynihan was a Fulbright fellow in London.

Moynihan was with the International Rescue Committee in 1954, and held a succession of secretarial posts in the New York governor's office from 1955 to 1958. Moynihan moved to Washington, D.C., in 1961, where he served as a labor advisor during the Kennedy and Johnson administrations until 1966. From 1966 to 1969 he was director of the Joint Center for Urban Studies of MIT and Harvard University.

Moynihan returned to Washington in 1970 as assistant for urban affairs to President Richard Nixon, serving as a counselor to the president and as a member of the Cabinet until 1976. A member of the U.S. delegation to the United Nations in 1971, he was appointed U.S. ambassador to India in 1973, and was the U.S. permanent representative to the UN from 1975 to 1976. Moynihan entered the political arena in 1977, serving as U.S. senator from New York. He has been chairman of the Senate Financial Committee since 1993.

Moynihan's books include *Maximum Feasible Misunderstanding* (1969), *Counting Our Blessings* (1980), and *On the Law of Nations* (1990). He has received honorary degrees and tributes in recognition of his long political and diplomatic career, and is the recipient of innumerable awards, including the American Philosophical Society's Hubert Humphrey Award in 1983, and its Thomas Jefferson Medal in 1993.

Senators Moynihan and Javits enjoyed a friendship that spanned three decades. As senator from New York, Javits was Moynihan's senior colleague when Moynihan entered that body as a freshman senator in 1977.

Eulogy for Jacob Javits by Senator Daniel P. Moynihan

"Let us now praise famous men and our fathers that begat us." Thus from Ecclesiastes, whose author describes himself as "king in Jerusalem" and whose thoughts commend themselves to us on this day that we remember Jacob Koppel Javits.

For as we think of him, now radiantly a part of our history, we do well to think of the history, the ideas, the devotions he brought to his triumphant and, at the end, transcendent life. Of these, none was more central than the Judaic truth that the quest for justice is the greatest of man's works, and the equally Judaic thought that his work never ends.

"And, indeed, I have observed under the sun: Alongside justice there is wickedness, alongside righteousness, there is wickedness." Hence, we learn of the inevitability of oppression, of evil. "The events that occur under the sun" God has brought to pass. "Even love! Even hate!"

"I realize," Ecclesiastes continues, "That whatever God has brought to pass will recur evermore . . . and God has brought it to pass that we revere Him."

I think especially of these words as I consider my years in the Senate with Jacob Javits. I was his junior colleague, and while we had known each other just under a third of a century as of Friday, he was in every sense my elder, and I would refer to him as "my revered senior colleague." A word to be used sparingly, and only for those whose lives reveal a reverence also, above all a reverence for life as God has given it to man: with all its testing and sorrow and appointed end.

He did not go gentle into that good night. Yea, he raged against the dying of the light and went luminously, gracefully; an example to the end. Others will now speak of the man they knew and loved. I take my leave. Jack: L'chaim.

Lyndon B. Johnson

August 27, 1908 ~ January 22, 1973

Eulogy delivered by Dean Rusk at a memorial service in the Capitol Rotunda, Washington, D.C., January 24, 1973

Lyndon B. Johnson

Lyndon Baines Johnson, thirty-sixth president of the United States, was born in Stonewall, Texas, the son of Samuel and Rebekah (Baines) Johnson. He earned a B.S. in 1930 from Southwest Texas State Teachers College in San Marcos, Texas, and received a doctorate in law from Southwestern University in 1943.

Johnson married Claudia Alta (Lady Bird) Taylor in 1934, and the couple had two daughters, Linda Bird and Lucy Baines. During World War II, he was a commander in the U.S. Naval Reserve, and saw active duty from 1941 to 1942. He was decorated with the Silver Star.

Johnson's political career began in 1937, when he was elected to Congress as a representative for Texas; he later served as senator from 1949 to 1961. He was named Senate minority leader in 1953, and majority leader in 1954. Johnson was vice president from 1961 until 1963, when he assumed the presidency on November 22 upon the assassination of President John F. Kennedy. In 1964, running against Republican Barry Goldwater, Johnson was elected president by an overwhelming margin, giving him a mandate for his social programs.

Johnson's presidency was characterized by far-reaching domestic triumphs and deepening foreign tragedy. Working with Congress to implement what he called the Great Society, Johnson secured such programs as Medicare and federal aid to education, as well as important civil rights legislation—the Civil Rights Act of 1964, and the Voting Rights Act of 1965. Despite these achievements, Johnson's policy of military escalation in Vietnam marred his effectiveness as president and, in the end, proved to be his undoing as the nation's leader.

Johnson left the presidency in 1969, and returned to Texas to write. His many books include *My Hope for America* (1964), *The Choices*

We Face (1968), and his memoirs, *The Vantage Point: Perspectives of the Presidency, 1963–1969* (1971).

Johnson is buried in the family cemetery in Stonewall, Texas.

Dean Rusk

Former U.S. secretary of state Dean Rusk was born on a farm in Cherokee County, Georgia, on February 9, 1909. During the Depression he put himself through Davidson College in North Carolina, earning a Rhodes scholarship to Oxford University in 1933, where he studied international relations, history, law, politics, and philosophy.

Rusk served in the Army during World War II, and joined the State Department in 1946. He was appointed assistant secretary for Far Eastern affairs in 1950.

Rusk left the government in 1952 to head the Ford Foundation, where he maintained an interest in Asia. He resigned from the foundation in 1960, and returned to Washington as secretary of state for the Kennedy administration. He remained at that post throughout the Johnson years as well.

During one of the nation's most turbulent eras both at home and abroad, Rusk used a firm diplomatic hand in handling such events as the Cuban Missile Crisis and the Vietnam War. While remaining a staunch defender of American policy in Vietnam, he received increasing criticism from Congress and the general public during his final years at the State Department. In 1963, amid the tensions of the Cold War, Rusk helped bring about the partial nuclear test ban treaty between the United States and the Soviet Union.

In 1970, Rusk returned to Georgia as the Sibley Professor of International Law at the University of Georgia at Athens, and retired in 1984. He died on December 20, 1994 at age eighty-five.

Dean Rusk was a friend of Lyndon Johnson, and served as his secretary of state.

Eulogy for Lyndon B. Johnson by Dean Rusk

A home on the bank of the Pedernales in the beautiful hill country of Texas, surrounded by his beloved family and the friends with whom he so fully shared his warm and generous spirit.

A home in this place where we are gathered today, in the Congress, which was his life for so long, filled with friendships and livened by that political debate which is the lifeblood of a free society, but friendships cemented by the common task of ensuring that the public business somehow would go forward at the end of the day.

A home for more than five years at the summit of responsibility, of responsibility and not necessarily of power—for he, as other presidents, understood that many expectations and demands were addressed to him which were beyond his constitutional reach or, indeed, beyond the reach of our nation in a world community where we might persuade but cannot command. These were years of awesome burdens, but burdens lightened by the fine intelligence and the natural grace and the personal devotion of the First Lady who was always at his side.

And now he returns to the Pedernales to a home among the immortals, that goodly company of men and women whom we shall forever cherish because they were concerned about those matters which barred the path to our becoming what we have in us to become.

More than a thousand years ago, in a simpler and more robust age, perhaps we might have known him as Lyndon the Liberator, for he was determined to free our people in body, mind, and spirit.

A few strokes of the brush cannot portray this man whom we offer our affections and respect today. As for me, I would begin with his deep compassion for his fellow man, a compassion which was shared by the Congress and resulted in the most extraordinary legislative season in our history.

Who can forget that remarkable evening of March 15, 1965, when President Johnson addressed a joint session of Congress on voting rights and other civil rights? It was perhaps his finest single message.

You will remember that, after recalling his days as a teacher of poor Mexican American children back in 1928, he said, "It never even occurred to me in my fondest dreams that I might have the chance to help people like them all over the country."

And then, with eyes which bored into the conscience of all who heard him, he said, "But now I do have that chance, and I'll let you in on a secret—I mean to use it. And I hope you will use it with me."

And then he went on to disclose in a very frank way what some of his deepest hopes were. Congressman Pickle has already quoted those hopes. One may give these ideas any name or epithet one might choose. They did not evolve out of some empty intellectual exercise. They were not the product of shrewd political calculation. His colleagues knew them as a volcanic eruption from the innermost being of his soul when the responsibility for leadership finally became his own.

Many have said that Lyndon Johnson was demanding upon his

colleagues and personal staff. Indeed he was. And demanding upon the Congress and the American people and many a foreign leader as well. But he was most demanding upon himself and stubbornly resisted the admonitions of his associates to slow down. There was so much to do, and there was so little time in which to get it done.

President Johnson sometimes deprecated his own background in foreign affairs. Actually, he brought great talents and a rich experience to this aspect of the presidency in November 1963. As senate majority leader throughout much of the Eisenhower years, he was necessarily and deeply involved in the widest range of legislation affecting foreign and defense policy.

When he became vice president, President Kennedy asked him frequently to make foreign visits and consult with foreign leaders on matters of major importance—not merely a tourist's visit.

He absorbed briefings in a most expert fashion, and with a powerful intellect went directly to the heart of the issues under discussion. And as many present know, he was always formidable in a negotiation or persuasion.

He had a special ability, perhaps learned in the Senate, to begin his consideration of a problem by putting himself in the other fellow's shoes, in an attempt to understand which answers might be possible.

He had a personal code of relations among political leaders which did not permit him or his colleagues to engage in personal vilification aimed at foreign leaders, however deep the disagreement might appear to be.

Today's writers are inclined to discuss Lyndon Johnson almost solely in terms of Vietnam, and such questions as whether he did too much or too little in that tragic struggle. The historian will take a broader view and weigh such things as the consular and civil air agreements with the Soviet Union, the nonproliferation treaty, our space treaties, his east-west trade bill, the beginnings of SALT talks, and many other initiatives aimed at building the peace.

He had a very special and affectionate feeling for the nations of the western hemisphere. He used to say to us, "This hemisphere is where we live, this is our home, these are our neighbors. We must start with our own neighborhood."

Mr. President [Richard Nixon], last evening you made some moving remarks about President Johnson in your brief address to the American people. We congratulate you on the substance of that address and give you our best wishes for the weeks and months ahead. I mention two points which you made about Lyndon Johnson. That President Johnson was a man of peace and would have welcomed the peace which seems now to be opening up in Southeast Asia. How true. And he would, indeed, have joined you, Mr. President, in paying tribute to those millions of gallant and dedicated men in uniform whose service and sacrifice opened the way for the peace which is before us. In his last State of the Union message to the Congress, his final sentence was, "But I believe that at least it will be said that we tried." Ah, yes, he tried, with reckless disregard for his own life.

And then, in the final chapter of his book, when he was reflecting upon how it looked to him as he returned to that ranch which he loved so much, his final sentence was, "And I knew also that I had given it everything that was in me."

As time passes, the world will increasingly acknowledge that the "everything" that was in him was a very great deal, and that men and women all over the earth are forever in his debt.

John F. Kennedy

May 29, 1917 ~ November 22, 1963

Tribute by Senator Jacob Javits at a memorial service in the Senate and appearing as a part of the *Congressional Record*

John F. Kennedy

The thirty-fifth president of the United States, John Fitzgerald Kennedy was born in Brookline, Massachusetts, to Joseph P. and Rose (Fitzgerald) Kennedy. He graduated from Harvard in 1940, and in that year his thesis on Britain's unpreparedness for war was published as *Why England Slept*. During the Second World War he served as a torpedo boat commander in the Pacific and was awarded the Navy Medal and the Purple Heart. Kennedy married Jacqueline Bouvier in 1953 and they had three children: Caroline, John Jr., and a second son who died in infancy.

A Democrat, he was first elected representative (1947) and then senator (1952) for Massachusetts. Plagued by serious back ailments in 1954 and 1955, he worked on a book during his recuperation. *Profiles in Courage* was published in 1956, and won the Pulitzer Prize for biography in 1957.

In 1960, Kennedy was the first Roman Catholic and the youngest president ever elected, winning by the smallest majority of the popular vote ever. In domestic affairs, the conservatism of Congress stalled many of his plans for a "new frontier" in social legislation. With his brother, Attorney General Robert Kennedy, he supported federal desegregation policy in schools and universities, and promoted further civil rights legislation. Abroad, Kennedy's administration suffered a setback in 1961 when anti-Castro Cubans, under the training and direction of the Central Intelligence Agency, failed in the Bay of Pigs invasion of Cuba. He displayed firmness and moderation in October 1962 when, at the risk of nuclear war, he induced the Soviet Union to withdraw its missiles from Cuba. Following this crisis, Kennedy achieved a partial nuclear test ban treaty with the Soviet Union in 1963.

On November 22, 1963, Kennedy was assassinated by rifle fire while riding in a motorcade through Dallas, Texas.

Jacob Javits

For a biographical sketch, see the eulogy for Jacob Javits, page 59. Senator Javits was a longtime friend and colleague of President Kennedy; they entered Congress on the same day in January 1947.

Tribute for John F. Kennedy by Jacob Javits

Mr. President, hundreds of thousands of words have been published, and hundreds of thousands more have been spoken into the microphones of the world since John F. Kennedy was struck down in Dallas, but none of them were really adequate. Words never are in the face of senseless tragedy.

Words cannot describe how the American people felt when they lost their president. Not until the vacuum of disbelief was filled with the horror of comprehension did any of us realize how much we identified ourselves, even apart from personal friendship, with the president—this intellectual, vigorous young man—and he would have been that if he were eighty—expressing the very essence of the youthfulness of our nation. It seems of little consequence now that there were political differences, or objections to this or that legislative product, though as far as I am concerned there was a very large measure of agreement. What matters is that feeling of loss—that personal sense of emptiness—that all Americans feel because their president was cut off in the prime of life. As a nation, we have lost a president who understood the institution of the presidency, gloried in its overwhelming responsibilities, and discharged his duties with dash and joy, which were an inspiration to the youth of our nation.

But John F. Kennedy was more than that. He was a man filled with the joy of living. He was a husband, a father—and my friend.

For myself, I remember coming to Congress the same day he did. We were sworn in together on the same January day in 1947. A photograph on my office wall shows that we two, returning veterans, looked a little uncomfortable at the moment in our civilian clothes. It shows us looking at the Taft-Ellender-Wagner housing bill, and it recalls the first job we did together when we called on the National Veterans Housing Conference of 1947, which we had organized, to back this bill. It was the beginning of an association which extended throughout our careers in the

House and Senate. We collaborated in many bipartisan matters, as is not unusual in the Congress. Indeed, in our service together in the Senate Committee on Labor and Public Welfare, we worked closely—as did Senator Morse and others—on the minimum wage bill, the Labor-Management Disclosure Act, and other similar measures which were major aspects of Senator Kennedy's legislative career.

I am a personal witness to the fact that he was resourceful, optimistic, and creative. He became and was my friend, and this is a deep source of gratification to me and to Mrs. Javits and our family.

Mrs. Javits, too, knew President Kennedy well and admired him greatly. She will, I know, always think of the president's graciousness and the warmth of personal friendship which he exuded.

Only a week before his tragic passing, I saw him in the Oval Room at the White House when he accepted the report of the Advisory Committee on Medical Care for the Aged, in which Senator Anderson and I joined, and issued a statement offering encouragement and help.

He was vigorous and healthy and smiling and friendly—a complete human being, concerned about other human beings who were no longer as vigorous and not quite as healthy as they used to be.

This concern for the unfortunate by a man with all of the social graces and all the social status and as much power as America allows one man was what made him so much the symbol of the youth of our country. His wife, Jacqueline, who has given Americans so much reason to be very proud of her and of all American womanhood as she reflected it, in these last mournful weeks, in the way she carried herself, has said the most beautiful tribute—that John F. Kennedy had the "hero idea of history," and that she did not want people to forget John F. Kennedy—the man—and replace him with some shadowy figure in the history books.

She need not fear that. There are already thousands upon thousands of people in the world working to keep his memory alive. I have been privileged to join with many others in this body in cosponsoring a bill to rename the National Cultural Center and make it a living, vibrant memorial to this vibrant man who loved the arts. And with Senator Humphrey, I have joined in a bill establishing a commission to ensure that only the most appropriate memorials be created in his honor.

These are well-meaning, deeply sincere tokens—necessary, but still tokens. In reality it will be John F. Kennedy's youthful freshness in his aspirations for our country that will keep his memory fresh.

In a real sense we, his former colleagues in the Congress, are the only ones with the power to write words which can transform these aspirations into memorials with meaning. We can write legislative acts, like a meaningful civil rights law, which would consecrate and perpetuate

John F. Kennedy's love for personal and national dignity. We can exorcize from our country—and the American people are doing that even now—those extremes of hatred and disbelief in public affairs which create a climate in which terrible acts become much more likely.

Acts such as these will be his final memorials. It is within our power to establish them. Perhaps his noblest memorial is that he would have wanted such memorials almost as no others.

So, in common with my colleagues in this solemn service—and that is what this is today—I bespeak for Mrs. Javits and my children—and I would place their names in the *Record,* so that as they read this *Record* when they grow up, I hope they will read their names in it and see that their father spoke with deep sympathy—Joy, Joshua, and Carla, to Mrs. Kennedy and the children, and to the president's father and mother and his brothers and sisters and their families our deepest sympathy on this terrible bereavement, for our nation and for all mankind, and in the deep expectation that flowers will grow from his grave for the benefit of man.

Robert Kennedy

November 20, 1928 ~ June 6, 1968

Eulogy delivered by Senator Edward Kennedy

Robert Kennedy

Robert Francis (Bobby) Kennedy was born in Boston to Joseph P. and Rose (Fitzgerald) Kennedy. He received a bachelor of arts from Harvard in 1948, and graduated from the University of Virginia Law School in 1951. Kennedy married Ethel Skakel in 1950, and the couple had eleven children.

Kennedy was named assistant counsel to Senator Joseph McCarthy's Permanent Investigations Subcommittee in 1953, and remained with that panel until 1956. In 1957, Kennedy was appointed chief counsel for the Senate Rackets Committee on improper activities in labor, and exposed corruption in the Teamsters' Union.

Kennedy managed the presidential campaign for his brother, John F. Kennedy, in 1960, and in 1961 he was named attorney general. In that capacity, Kennedy stressed enforcement of civil rights, and became his brother's closest advisor. During this period, Kennedy wrote two books, *The Enemy Within* (1960) and *Pursuit of Justice* (1964).

After John Kennedy's assassination, Robert Kennedy resigned as attorney general and won a U.S. Senate seat from New York, where he became recognized as a voice for the rights of minorities. An outspoken critic of the Vietnam War and an advocate for social reform, he ran for the Democratic presidential nomination in 1968.

Robert F. Kennedy was assassinated in Los Angeles in June 1968, following his victory in the California primary.

Edward Kennedy

Senator Edward (Ted) Moore Kennedy, younger brother of John F. and Robert F. Kennedy, was born in Boston on February 22, 1932, the son of Joseph P. and Rose (Fitzgerald) Kennedy. Kennedy was awarded an A.B. from Harvard in 1956, and an LL.B. from the University of Virginia Law

School in 1959. He married Joan Kennedy, with whom he has three children; after a divorce, he married Victoria Anne Reggie in 1992.

From 1961 to 1962 Kennedy served as assistant district attorney for Suffolk County, Massachusetts. In 1962 he was elected U.S. senator from Massachusetts, a position he has held until the present. A leader of the liberal Democrats in the Senate, he has served as chairman of the Senate Judiciary Committee (1979 to 1981), and as the ranking Democratic member of the Labor and Human Resources Committee since 1981. He has often been considered the leading Democratic contender for the presidential nomination, but entered the race only once in 1980, when he challenged the incumbent, Jimmy Carter. Since losing that race, Kennedy has remained in the Senate as a leading advocate of social reform.

Kennedy is the author of several books, including *Decisions for a Decade* (1968) and *In Critical Condition: The Crisis in America's Health Care* (1972). He has been the president of the Joseph P. Kennedy Jr. Foundation since 1961, and is also a trustee of Children's Hospital Medical Center of Boston, the John F. Kennedy Library, the John F. Kennedy Center for the Performing Arts, and the Robert F. Kennedy Memorial Foundation.

He is the recipient of numerous awards and citations from such organizations as the U.S. Committee for Refugees, the American Immigration and Citizenship Council, and the Leadership Conference on Civil Rights.

Eulogy for Robert Kennedy by Edward Kennedy

On behalf of Mrs. Robert Kennedy, her children, and the parents and sisters of Robert Kennedy, I want to express what we feel to those who mourn with us today in this cathedral and around the world.

We loved him as a brother and father and son. From his parents, and from his older brothers and sisters—Joe, Kathleen, and Jack—he received inspiration which he passed on to all of us. He gave us strength in time of trouble, wisdom in time of uncertainty, and sharing in time of happiness. He was always by our side.

Love is not an easy feeling to put into words. Nor is loyalty, or trust or joy. But he was all of these. He loved life completely and lived it intensely.

A few years back, Robert Kennedy wrote some words about his own father and they expressed the way we in his family feel about him. He said of what his father meant to him:

> What it really all adds up to is love—not love as it is described with much facility in popular magazines, but the kind of love that is affection and respect, order, encouragement, and support. Our awareness of this was an incalculable source of strength, and because real love is something unselfish and involves sacrifice and giving, we could not help but profit from it.
>
> Beneath it all, he has tried to engender a social conscience. There were wrongs which needed attention. There were people who were poor and who needed help. And we have a responsibility to them and to this country. Through no virtues and accomplishments on our part, we have been fortunate enough to be born in the United States under the most comfortable conditions. We, therefore, have a responsibility to others who are less well off.

This is what Robert Kennedy was given. What he leaves us is what he said, what he did, and what he stood for. A speech he made to the young people of South Africa on their Day of Affirmation in 1966 sums it up the best, and I would read it now:

> There is a discrimination in this world and slavery and slaughter and starvation. Governments repress their people; and millions are trapped in poverty while the nation grows rich; and wealth is lavished on armaments everywhere.
>
> There are differing evils, but they are the common works of man. They reflect the imperfection of human justice, the inadequacy of human compassion, our lack of sensibility toward the sufferings of our fellows.
>
> But we can perhaps remember—even if only for a time—that those who live with us are our brothers, that they share with us the same short moment of life; that they seek—as we do—nothing but the chance to live out their lives in purpose and happiness, winning what satisfaction and fulfillment they can.
>
> Surely this bond of common faith, this bond of common goal, can begin to teach us something. Surely we can learn, at least, to look at those around us as fellow men. And surely we can begin to work a little harder to bind up the wounds among us and to become in our own hearts brothers and countrymen once again.
>
> Our answer is to rely on youth—not a time of life but a state of mind, a temper of the will, a quality of imagination, a predominance of courage over timidity, of the appetite for adventure over the love of ease. The cruelties and obstacles of this swiftly changing planet will not yield to obsolete dogmas and outworn slogans. They cannot be moved by those who cling to a present that is already dying, who prefer the illusion of security to the excitement and danger that comes with even the most peaceful progress. It is a revolutionary world we live in; and this generation, at home and around the world, has had thrust upon it a greater burden of responsibility than any generation that has ever lived.

Some believe there is nothing one man or one woman can do against the enormous array of the world's ills. Yet many of the world's greatest movements, of thought and action, have flowed from the work of a single man. A young monk began the Protestant Reformation, a young general extended an empire from Macedonia to the borders of the earth, and a young woman reclaimed the territory of France. It was a young Italian explorer who discovered the New World, and the thirty-two-year-old Thomas Jefferson who proclaimed that all men are created equal.

These men moved the world, and so can we all. Few will have the greatness to bend history itself, but each of us can work to change a small portion of events, and in the total of all those acts will be written the history of this generation. It is from numberless diverse acts of courage and belief that human history is shaped. Each time a man stands up for an ideal, or acts to improve the lot of others, or strikes out against injustice, he sends forth a tiny ripple of hope, and crossing each other from a million different centers of energy and daring those ripples build a current that can sweep down the mightiest walls of oppression and resistance.

Few are willing to brave the disapproval of their fellows, the censure of their colleagues, the wrath of their society. Moral courage is a rarer commodity than bravery in battle or great intelligence. Yet it is the one essential, vital quality for those who seek to change a world that yields most painfully to change. And I believe that in this generation those with the courage to enter the moral conflict will find themselves with companions in every corner of the globe.

For the fortunate among us, there is the temptation to follow the easy and familiar paths of personal ambition and financial success so grandly spread before those who enjoy the privilege of education. But that is not the road history has marked out for us. Like it or not, we live in times of danger and uncertainty. But they are also more open to the creative energy of men than any other time in history. All of us will ultimately be judges and as the years pass we will surely judge ourselves on the effort we have contributed to building a new world society and the extent to which our ideals and goals have shaped that effort.

The future does not belong to those who are content with today, apathetic toward common problems and their fellow man alike, timid and fearful in the face of new ideas and bold projects. Rather it will belong to those who can blend vision, reason, and courage in a personal commitment to the ideals and great enterprises of American society.

Our future may lie beyond our vision, but is not completely beyond our control. It is the shaping impulse of America that neither fate nor nature nor the irresistible tides of history, but the work of our own hands, matched to reason and principle, will determine our destiny. There is pride in that, even arrogance, but there is also experience and truth. In any event, it is the only way we can live.

This is the way he lived. My brother need not be idealized, or enlarged in death beyond what he was in life, to be remembered simply as a good and decent man, who saw wrong and tried to right it, saw suffering and tried to heal it, saw war and tried to stop it.

Those of us who loved him and who take him to his rest today pray that what he was to us and what he wished for others will someday come to pass for all the world.

As he said many times, in many parts of this nation, to those he touched and who sought to touch him:

> "Some men see things as they are and say why.
> I dream things that never were and say why not."

Martin Luther King Jr.

January 15, 1929 ~ April 4, 1968

Eulogy delivered by Benjamin E. Mays,
Morehouse College, Atlanta, Georgia,
April 9, 1968

Martin Luther King Jr.

The American clergyman and civil rights leader Martin Luther King Jr. was born in Atlanta, Georgia. The son of a Baptist pastor, he received a bachelor's degree in sociology from Morehouse College (1948), a B.D. from Crozier Theological Seminary (1951), and a doctorate in philosophy from Boston University (1955). He married Coretta Scott King in 1953.

In 1954, King became minister of a Baptist church in Montgomery, Alabama. During 1955 and 1956, he gained national prominence as leader of the Alabama bus boycott. Following that success, he founded the Southern Christian Leadership Conference, which organized civil rights activities throughout the country. His first book, *Stride Toward Freedom,* was published in 1958. A brilliant orator, King galvanized the civil rights movement, which was based on the principle of nonviolence. He led the great March on Washington in 1963, where he delivered his memorable "I Have a Dream" speech. His second book, *Why We Can't Wait,* was published in 1964, and later that year he was awarded the Nobel Peace Prize.

In 1965 King led a tortuous march from Selma to Montgomery as part of a voter-registration drive. After 1965, his speeches increasingly reflected his growing understanding of the relationship between economics and racism, and he began to speak out against the war in Vietnam.

King was assassinated in Memphis, Tennessee, on April 4, 1968, while on a trip to lend support to striking sanitation workers. His family has carried on his work through the Martin Luther King Jr. Center for Social Change in Alabama. King's birthday was declared a federal holiday in 1983—the third Monday in January is celebrated as Martin Luther King Day.

Benjamin E. Mays

American educator Benjamin Elijah Mays was born in Epworth, South Carolina, on August 1, 1894. The son of Hezekiah and Louvenia (Carter) Mays, he married Sadie Gray in 1926. Mays graduated with honors from South Carolina State College in 1920, and received an M.A. (1925) and a Ph.D. (1935) from the University of Chicago. He also received a doctorate in law from Denison University of Granville, Ohio, in 1945, and a doctor of divinity from Bates College in Lewiston, Maine, in 1947.

Mays was dean of Howard University's Divinity School from 1934 to 1940, and president of Morehouse College from 1940 to 1967. From 1967 to 1981 he served on the Atlanta, Georgia, board of education. A strong proponent of civil rights, he opposed militants and inspired Martin Luther King Jr. in his nonviolent approach to civil disobedience.

Mays was the author of several books, including *The Negro's Church* (1933), *Seeking to Be Christian in Race Relations* (1957), *Disturbed about Man* (1969), and his autobiography, *Born to Rebel* (1971).

Mays died at his home in Atlanta, Georgia, on March 28, 1984.

Dr. Mays was a close friend of Dr. King from the time Martin Luther King Jr. was a student at Morehouse College during Mays's tenure as college president.

Eulogy for Martin Luther King Jr. by Benjamin E. Mays

To be honored by being requested to give the eulogy at the funeral of Dr. Martin Luther King Jr. is like asking one to eulogize his deceased son—so close and so precious was he to me. Our friendship goes back to his student days at Morehouse College. It is not an easy task; nevertheless I accept it, with a sad heart and with full knowledge of my inadequacy to do justice to this man. It was my desire that if I predeceased Dr. King, he would pay tribute to me on my final day. It was his wish that if he predeceased me, I would delivery the homily at his funeral. Fate has decreed that I eulogize him. I wish it might have been otherwise, for, after all, I am three score and ten and Martin Luther is dead at thirty-nine.

Although there are some who rejoice in his death, there are millions across the length and breadth of this world who are smitten with grief that this friend of mankind—all mankind—has been cut down in the flower of his youth. So, multitudes here and in foreign lands, queens, kings, heads of governments, the clergy of the world, and the common man everywhere, are praying that God will be with the family, the American people, and the president of the United States in this tragic hour. We hope that this universal concern will bring comfort to the family—for grief is like a heavy load: when shared it is easier to bear. We come today to help the family carry the load.

We have assembled here from every section of this great nation and from other parts of the world to give thanks to God that He gave to America, at this moment in history, Martin Luther King Jr. Truly God is no respecter of persons. How strange! God called the grandson of a slave on his father's side, and the grandson of a man born during the Civil War on his mother's side, and said to him: "Martin Luther, speak to America about war and peace; about social justice and racial discrimination; about its obligation to the poor; and about nonviolence as a way of perfecting social change in a world of brutality and war."

Here was a man who believed with all of his might that the pursuit of violence at any time is ethically and morally wrong; that God and the moral weight of the universe are against it; that violence is self-defeating; and that only love and forgiveness can break the vicious circle of revenge. He believed that nonviolence would prove effective in the abolition of injustice in politics, in economics, in education, and in race relations. He was convinced, also, that people could not be moved to abolish voluntarily the inhumanity of man to man by mere persuasion and pleading, but that they could be moved to do so by dramatizing the evil through massive nonviolent resistance. He believed that nonviolent direct action was necessary to supplement the nonviolent victories in the federal courts. He believed that the nonviolent approach to solving social problems would ultimately prove to be redemptive.

Out of this conviction, history records the marches in Montgomery, Birmingham, Selma, Chicago, and other cities. He gave people an ethical and moral way to engage in activities designed to perfect social change without bloodshed and violence; and when violence did erupt it was that which is potential in any protest which aims to uproot deeply entrenched wrongs. No reasonable person would deny that the activities and the personality of Martin Luther King Jr. contributed largely to the success of the student sit-in movements; in abolishing segregation in downtown establishments; and that his activities contributed mightily to the passage of the civil rights legislation of 1964 and 1965.

Martin Luther King Jr. believed in a united America; that the walls of separation brought on by legal and de facto segregation and discrimination based on race and color could be eradicated. As he said in his Washington monument address: "I have a dream."

He had faith in his country. He died striving to desegregate and integrate America to the end that this great nation of ours, born in revolution and blood, conceived in liberty and dedicated to the proposition that all men are created free and equal, will truly become the lighthouse of freedom where none will be denied because his skin is black and none favored because his eyes are blue; where our nation will be militarily strong but perpetually at peace; economically secure but just; learned but wise; where the poorest—the garbage collectors—will have bread enough and to spare; where no one will be poorly housed; each educated up to his capacity; and where the richest will understand the meaning of empathy. This was his dream, and the end toward which he strove. As he and his followers often sang: "We shall overcome someday; black and white together."

Let it be thoroughly understood that our deceased brother did not embrace nonviolence out of fear or cowardice. Moral courage was one of his noblest virtues. As Mahatma Gandhi challenged the British Empire without a sword and won, Martin Luther King Jr. challenged the interracial wrongs of his country without a gun. And he had the faith to believe that he would win the battle for social justice. I make bold to assert that it took more courage for King to practice nonviolence than it took his assassin to fire the fatal shot. The assassin is a coward: he committed his dastardly deed and fled. When Martin Luther disobeyed an unjust law, he accepted the consequences of his actions. He never ran away and he never begged for mercy. He returned to the Birmingham jail to serve his time.

Perhaps he was more courageous than soldiers who fight and die on the battlefield. There is an element of compulsion in their dying. But when Martin Luther faced death again and again, and finally embraced it, there was no external pressure. He was acting on an inner compulsion that drove him on. More courageous than those who advocate violence as a way out, for they carry weapons of destruction for defense. But Martin Luther faced the dogs, the police, jail, heavy criticism, and finally death; and he never carried a gun, not even a knife to defend himself. He had only his faith in a just God to rely on; and the belief that "thrice is he armed who has his quarrels just." The faith that Browning writes about when he says: "One who never turned his back, but marched abreast forward; Never doubted that clouds would break; Never dreamed that right though worsted wrong would triumph; Held we fall to rise, are baffled to fight better; Sleep to wake."

Coupled with moral courage was Martin Luther King Jr.'s capacity to love people. Though deeply committed to a program of freedom for Negroes, he had love and concern for all kinds of peoples. He drew no distinction between the high and the low; none between the rich and the poor. He believed especially that he was sent to champion the cause of the man farthest down. He would probably say that if death had to come,

I am sure there was no greater cause to die for than fighting to get a just wage for garbage collectors. He was suprarace, supranation, supradenomination, supraclass, and supraculture. He belonged to the world and to mankind. Now he belongs to posterity.

But there is a dichotomy in all this. This man was loved by some and hated by others. If any man knew the meaning of suffering, King knew. House bombed; living day by day for thirteen years under constant threats of death; maliciously accused of being a Communist; falsely accused of being insincere and seeking the limelight for his own glory; stabbed by a member of his own race; slugged in a hotel lobby; jailed thirty times; occasionally deeply hurt because friends betrayed him—and yet this man had no bitterness in his heart, no rancor in his soul, no revenge in his mind; and he went up and down the length and breadth of this world preaching nonviolence and the redemptive power of love. He believed with all his heart, mind, and soul that the way to peace and brotherhood is through nonviolence, love, and suffering. He was severely criticized for his opposition to the war in Vietnam. It must be said, however, that one could hardly expect a prophet of Dr. King's commitments to advocate nonviolence at home and violence in Vietnam. Nonviolence to King was total commitment not only in solving the problems of race in the United States but in solving the problems of the world.

Surely this man was called of God to do this work. If Amos and Micah were prophets in the eighth century B.C., Martin Luther King Jr. was a prophet in the twentieth century. If Isaiah was called of God to prophesy in his day, Martin Luther was called of God to prophesy in his time. If Hosea was sent to preach love and forgiveness centuries ago, Martin Luther was sent to expound the doctrine of nonviolence and forgiveness in the third quarter of the twentieth century. If Jesus was called to preach the Gospel to the poor, Martin Luther was called to give dignity to the common man. If a prophet is one who interprets in clear and intelligible language the will of God, Martin Luther King Jr. fits that designation. If a prophet is one who does not seek popular causes to espouse, but rather the causes he thinks are right, Martin Luther qualified on that score.

No! He was not ahead of his time. No man is ahead of his time. Every man is within his star, each in his time. Each man must respond to the call of God in his lifetime and not in somebody else's time. Jesus had to respond to the call of God in the first century A.D., and not in the twentieth century. He had but one life to live. He couldn't wait. How long do you think Jesus would have had to wait for the constituted authorities to accept him? Twenty-five years? A hundred years? A thousand? He died at thirty-three. He couldn't wait. Paul, Galileo, Copernicus, Martin

Luther the Protestant reformer, Gandhi and Nehru couldn't wait for another time. They had to act in their lifetimes. No man is ahead of his time. Abraham, leaving his country in obedience to God's call; Moses leading a rebellious people to the Promised Land; Jesus dying on a cross; Galileo on his knees recanting; Lincoln dying of an assassin's bullet; Woodrow Wilson crusading for a League of Nations; Martin Luther King Jr. dying fighting for justice for garbage collectors—none of these men were ahead of their time. With them the time was always ripe to do that which was right and that which needed to be done.

Too bad, you say, that Martin Luther King Jr. died so young. I feel that way, too. But, as I have said many times before, it isn't how long one lives, but how well. It's what one accomplishes for mankind that matters. Jesus died at thirty-three; Joan of Arc at nineteen; Byron and Burns at thirty-six; Keats and Marlow at twenty-nine; Shelly at thirty; Dunbar before thirty-five; John Fitzgerald Kennedy at forty-six; William Rainey Harper at forty-nine; and Martin Luther King Jr. at thirty-nine.

We all pray that the assassin will be apprehended and brought to justice. But, make no mistake, the American people are in part responsible for Martin Luther King Jr.'s death. The assassin heard enough condemnation of King and of Negroes to feel that he had public support. He knew that millions hated King.

The Memphis officials must bear some of the guilt for Martin Luther's assassination. The strike should have been settled several weeks ago. The lowest paid men in our society should not have to strike for a more just wage. A century after emancipation, and after the enactment of the Thirteenth, Fourteenth, and Fifteenth Amendments, it should not have been necessary for Martin Luther King Jr. to stage marches in Montgomery, Birmingham, and Selma, and go to jail thirty times trying to achieve for his people those rights which people of lighter hue get by virtue of their being born white. We, too, are guilty of murder. It is time for the American people to repent and make democracy equally applicable to all Americans. What can we do? We, and not the assassins, represent America at its best. We have the power—not the assassins—to make things right.

If we love Martin Luther King Jr. and respect him, as this crowd surely testifies, let us see to it that he did not die in vain; let us see to it that we do not dishonor his name by trying to solve our problems through rioting in the streets. Violence was foreign to his nature. He warned that continued riots could produce a fascist state. But let us see to it also that the conditions that cause riots are promptly removed, as the president of the United States is trying to get us to do. Let black and white alike search their hearts; and if there be prejudice in our hearts against any racial or ethnic group, let us exterminate it and let us pray, as Martin Luther King Jr. would pray if he could: Father, forgive them for they know not what they do. If we do this, Martin Luther King Jr. will have died a redemptive death from which all mankind will benefit.

Morehouse College will never be the same because Martin Luther came by here; and the nation and the world will be indebted to him for centuries to come. It is natural, therefore, that we are here at Morehouse and President Gloster would want to memorialize him to serve as an inspiration to all students who study in this Center.

I close by saying to you what Martin Luther King Jr. believed: If physical death was the price he had to pay to rid America of prejudice and injustice, nothing could be more redemptive. And, to paraphrase the words of the immortal John Fitzgerald Kennedy, permit me to say that Martin Luther King Jr.'s unfinished work on earth must truly be our own.

William Kunstler

July 7, 1919 ~ September 4, 1995

Eulogy delivered by Ronald L. Kuby

William Kunstler

American attorney William Moses Kunstler was born in New York City, the son of Monroe Bradford and Frances (Mandelbaum) Kunstler. He married Lottie Rosenberger in 1943. The couple had two children, and were divorced in 1975. He married Margaret L. Cohen in 1975, and together they had two children.

During the Second World War, Kunstler served with the U.S. Air Force in the Pacific, attained the rank of major, and was decorated with the Bronze Star. Kunstler received a bachelor of arts from Yale in 1941, and a bachelor of law from Columbia in 1948. In 1949 he became a partner with his brother in the New York City firm that became known as Kunstler, Kunstler, Hyman and Goldberg. From 1950 to 1992, he was associate professor of law at the New York Law School. From 1992 until his death he was a partner in the firm Kunstler & Kuby.

Kunstler was an adventurous lawyer who began taking controversial cases in the 1950s. He was a defender of civil rights defendants in the South during the early sixties, and gained his reputation as a "radical" during his defense of the Chicago Seven in 1968. Kunstler represented other high-profile defendants throughout his career, such as Malcolm X, Native American activist Leonard Peltier, the Berrigan brothers, and the convicts involved in the Attica, New York, prison riot.

Kunstler was the author of several books, including *The Case for Courage: The Stories of Ten Famous American Attorneys Who Risked Their Careers in the Cause of Justice* (1962) and *My Life as a Radical Lawyer* (1994). He was a member of the American Civil Liberties Union, serving as its director (1964 to 1970) and on its national council (1968 to 1995). During his career, Kunstler received numerous awards and honors, including the 1994 Thurgood Marshall Practitioner Award of the New York Association of Criminal Defense Lawyers.

Ronald L. Kuby

Ron Kuby was a law intern when he first met William Kunstler, who had been a radical lawyer for over twenty years. He became Kunstler's partner the next year, and himself took up the fight for the poor, the oppressed, and the downtrodden.

Kuby continued to represent the outcasts under the name of Kunstler and Kuby. He has represented some of the more newsworthy clients since Kunstler's passing, and continues to work in New York City.

Mr. Kuby was Mr. Kunstler's partner from the time he started to practice law, as well as his best friend.

Eulogy for William Kunstler by Ronald L. Kuby

Thirty-four years ago, William M. Kunstler, a lawyer with a traditional practice, received a telephone call from an ACLU representative. Lawyers were needed in Mississippi, the caller explained, to help defend the young people who were being arrested for riding the interstate buses in defiance of the segregation law. Bill Kunstler was one of the first and most daring of the "movement lawyers," a lawyer for the young causes of desegregation and civil rights. When the Freedom Riders faced trials in racist Southern state courts, he found a century-old law and removed those cases to the more liberal federal benches. He filed flurries of federal writs, neutralizing the segregationist state judges. His itinerant lawyering throughout the South helped ensure the survival of the civil rights movement.

As the movement to end the war in Vietnam came under mounting governmental attack, Bill Kunstler pioneered new methods of defense—bringing the streets into the courtroom, and the courtroom into the streets. While defending the Chicago Seven, he put the war in Vietnam on trial—asking Judy Collins to sing "Where Have All the Flowers Gone" from the witness stand, placing a Viet Cong flag on the defense table, and wearing a black armband to commemorate the war dead.

Critics sniffed that such tactics were just theatre. But that criticism came from the elitists who have always argued that history is made from the top down, by the judges and crowned kings, rather than by the damned and the Dr. Kings.

More than any other attorney, Bill Kunstler shattered the then-prevailing model of lawyerly detachment. He showed us that neutrality in the face of evil was not a virtue, and taught the legal profession that it really did matter which side it was on.

Bill Kunstler brought extraordinary courage to the practice of law. He stood up to the guns of racist Southern sheriffs. At the Attica prison rebellion in 1971, he risked his life trying desperately to help prevent a massacre. He received a staggering sentence of four years in federal prison for contempt of court—later reversed on appeal—in Chicago. The critics harrumphed that this was all "posturing." But these are the same critics who would have us believe that cowardice is really some exalted form of decorum.

Bill Kunstler's courage, his work, and his presence, inspired generations of lawyers, many of whom still labor for the poor and oppressed. They are a reminder that there was a time in America when William M. Kunstler would be on TV and young people would say: "That is what I want to do! That is who I want to be!" Few of Bill Kunstler's critics in the legal world have inspired anything but cynicism, or stood for anything grander than getting a big fee.

As a member of the generation that Bill Kunstler inspired, becoming his law partner was the greatest gift I have ever received. Even in the grimmest of times and in the most hopeless of fights, Bill Kunstler radiated love, passion, and joy. His compassion for the downtrodden was as boundless as his loathing of oppression. From the time he first shoved a cup of coffee in my hand when I was an eager law intern in 1982, until I said my final goodbye to him last week, Bill Kunstler lit up my life as he did the lives of so many others. The nation lost a hero—I have lost my best friend.

Bill Kunstler's contribution to the mind of American law was as great as his contribution to its heart. In a landmark case, he desegregated the Washington, D.C., schools. He won the flag-burning cases in the Supreme Court, expanding the protection of freedom of speech. He successfully struck down New York's death penalty law in 1984, giving all New Yorkers a decade free from state-sponsored murder. His recent, controversial jury verdicts—the El Sayyid Nosair and Larry Davis acquittals—were won through meticulous cross-examination and dry, technical lawyering. And he was always there for the thousands upon thousands of the dispossessed who found a way to his door. We are all a little freer, and a little safer, for his life as a radical lawyer.

Stan Laurel

June 16, 1890 ~ February 23, 1965

Eulogy delivered by Dick Van Dyke at the funeral

Stan Laurel

Comedian Arthur Stanley Jefferson Laurel was born in Ulverston, England. As a member of a vaudeville company that included Charlie Chaplin, he first came to the United States in 1910, eventually making his way to Hollywood. In 1917 he began work for the Hal Roach studio as a producer and director, and began his partnership with Oliver Hardy in 1926. Hardy had been destined for a legal career, but left college to join a troupe of minstrels before drifting into the film industry. From their first film together, they never worked apart.

Although Laurel is usually described as the more creative partner, the team was much funnier and more successful than its individual parts. They made nearly two hundred films—Laurel himself did most of the editing—but their early shorts are generally recognized as their best work. They survived the advent of the "talkies" better than many others, even though their style was basically silent. Purveying good honest slapstick, they deliberately avoided any attempt at subtlety. Ollie—fat, pretentious, and blustering—fiddled with his tie and appealed to the camera for help, while Stan—thin, bullied, and confused—scratched his head, looked blank, and dissolved into tears. Their contrasting personalities, general clumsiness and stupidity, and disaster-packed predicaments made them a universally popular comedy duo.

Dick Van Dyke

Actor and comedian Dick Van Dyke was born in West Plains, Missouri, on December 13, 1925. He married Marjorie Willett in 1948, and the couple have four children.

Beginning in school plays and civic theatre productions, Van Dyke's first professional work (1947 to 1953) was done in partnership with Philip Erickson in the pantomime act Eric and Van. He broke into television as a master of ceremonies for various shows throughout the 1950s, and after his success in the Broadway and film versions of the musical *Bye Bye Birdie,* he was given his own weekly comedy program, *The*

Dick Van Dyke Show (1961 to 1966). This was followed by *The New Dick Van Dyke Show* (1971 to 1974), and he performed on the weekly comedy program *The Carol Burnett Show* as well.

Van Dyke has appeared in various motion pictures, including *Mary Poppins* (1965), *Chitty, Chitty, Bang, Bang* (1968), and *Dick Tracy* (1990). In 1970 he authored the book *Faith, Hope and Hilarity*. In 1960 he was the recipient of the Theater World award, and in 1961 he was awarded the Antoinette Perry award for best musical comedy actor. He won Emmy awards for comedy in 1962, 1964, and 1965.

Mr. Van Dyke was a friend and longtime admirer of Stan Laurel.

Eulogy for Stan Laurel by Dick Van Dyke

Thirty years ago when the latest Laurel and Hardy movie played in my hometown in Illinois I attended the Saturday matinees; that is to say, from about 11:00 A.M. to maybe 9:00 or 10:00 P.M.—or whenever my mother and father came to drag me home.

From there on, and for the rest of the week, my parents were entertained, regaled, as were my friends at school by my impressions of Stan Laurel. But nobody really paid a lot of attention because every other kid on the block was doing his impressions of Stan Laurel. My father always did a pretty good impression of Stan. You would have to go to a far corner of the world to find somebody who doesn't do an impression of Stan Laurel.

There are hundreds of millions of people all over the world who felt the pang of sorrow and sadness when Stan left us, and it's impossible for anyone to speak for all of those people. All I can do is speak for myself and say how I felt about him. Stan's influence decided me to go into show business in the first place and his influence molded my point of view, my attitude about comedy. I never of course had met the man, but four years ago, when I came to California I meant to meet Stan Laurel by hook or crook and I wangled for a year, any way I could, to get his phone number, his address—anything that could put me in touch with him. Do you know where I finally found it? In the phone book . . . in a West Los Angeles phone book: Stan Laurel, Ocean Avenue, Santa Monica. A teenaged kid picked up the phone and received an invitation to come up there and visit, just the same as I did.

When Stan passed away, his little desk there was awash with fan mail that had been pouring in from all over the world as it had been during most of his later life; he insisted on sitting there, at that little portable typewriter and answering every one of them, personally, and of course he was so far back—months and months behind in the answering, but he wouldn't give up. He never gave up on anything; he never gave up on life and most of all, he never gave up that God-given mirth that he had.

In the wee small hours of one of his last mornings on earth, a nurse came into Stan's room to give him emergency aid. Stan looked up and said: "You know what—I'd lot rather be skiing." The nurse said, "Do you ski, Mr. Laurel?" He said: "No! But I'd lot rather be skiing than doing this."

Stan once remarked that Chaplin and Lloyd made all the big pictures and he and Babe made all the little cheap ones. "But they tell me," he said, "our little cheap ones have been seen by more people through the years than all the big ones. They must have seen how much love we put into them."

And that's what put Stan Laurel head and shoulders above all the rest of them—as an artist, and as a man. He put into his work that one special ingredient. He was a master comedian and he was a master artist—but he put in that one ingredient that can only come from the human being, and that was love. Love for his work, love for life, love for his audience, and how he loved that public. They were never squares or jerks to Stan Laurel.

Some of his contemporaries didn't criticize Stan favorably back in the thirties. Some of his contemporaries took great delight in showing their tools, and their skills, their methods, on the screen; they were applauded because the audience could see their art. Stan was never really applauded for his art because he took too much care to hide it, to conceal the hours of hard creative work that went into his movies. He didn't want you to see that—he just wanted you to laugh, and you did! You could never get him to pontificate about comedy. He was asked thousands of times, all through his life, to analyze comedy.

"What's funny?" he was always asked, and he always said: "How do I know? Can you analyze it? Can anybody?" He said: "All I know is just how to make people laugh."

That's all he knew!

Stan always believed that no comedy could merely depend on the spoken word, and all over the world, millions of people have laughed at Stan who never understood one word he ever said.

His sense of humor was clean and it was kind. The worst things that ever happened in a Laurel and Hardy movie happened to Stan Laurel.

Stan was the creative one of the team, and the Babe liked that very much. His leisure hours were spent on the golf course. He was an easy-going, extroverted, happy man, and that was the way Ollie liked it. Stan found his fulfillment in the free hours which he spent at the studio—he loved working on new gags, on new ideas for comedy. Comedy was his whole life. Ollie had one well-known answer when anybody asked him about any of their current projects; he always said: "Ask Stan."

And that's a piece of advice that was still being taken during the last few years by every great comedian in this country, and all the other countries around the world. They all came to "ask Stan." That living room in that small apartment has been graced in the last few years by Jerry Lewis, Danny Kaye, Marcel Marceau, Red Skelton, and dozens and dozens of others who just came up to "ask Stan." They all recognized him as the greatest of them all. His sweetness to me, I'll never forget. Stan didn't let them down either when they went up there. He was just as aware of the world around him in 1965 as he was at any other time in his life, and he knew what was funny about it—he saw what was funny about it too. And I can tell you, he could be the greatest today all over again.

I once tried to do an impression of Stan Laurel on my television show and I took meticulous care to get just the right kind of hat, the right kind of clothes, and to get everything down right. I put it on the air, and in a fever after the show, I called him up and said, "What did you think?" He said, "It was just fine, Dicky, but . . ." and for the next forty minutes, he gave me a list of details that I had done wrong. He was a perfectionist. And then he just said "God bless" and hung up. I wish I had a tape of that phone call: he said more things in there than I'll ever learn about my business, or the importance of human beings being able to laugh at themselves. A man like Stan Laurel taught millions and millions of people to laugh at themselves. Somehow when we lose a great leader, a great scientist, a great teacher, there always seems to be somebody to take their place. But the loss that we had with a man like Stan Laurel is a deep one because there doesn't seem to be anybody to take his place. He won't happen again because the world's a different place now.

Three generations of people found his comedy equally human, warm, and funny through his films, which he never owned, maybe future generations will; but he will never happen again and the world seems to know it. Telegrams and phone calls poured in from almost every country in the world, expressing love and affection and grief at the news that Stan had left us.

There were some strange places that Stan and Ollie went—they never took a vacation for a long time—but once they took a tourist vacation and went to China. They were in the deepest, deepest part of the interior of China and, as tourists, they visited a Buddhist temple there. They were invited to come in and look at the altar, and there on the altar was a tremendous blow-up in color of Ollie and Stan.

Once when they were in England—on a tour—they were surprised to find that wherever they went they were mobbed by crowds of people. They didn't realize how much everyone loved them so. They were hiding in Cobh, Ireland, to get some quiet, and suddenly, the church bells of Cobh began to ring—playing the *Cuckoo Song* and Stan said, "We both cried at that time, because of the love we felt coming from everyone."

Stan, of course, as most people know, spent the last years of his life with a serious illness. Those years were shared by his wonderful wife, Ida. She was the only one who really knew about the pain and suffering that was behind that famous smile, that wonderful high-pitched giggle he had. She shared his memories with him. He has a daughter, of course, Lois, and a son-in-law, Rand, and two grandchildren who had a better grandfather than Santa Claus could have been.

Stan and Ollie are both gone now and I feel the halls of heaven must be ringing with divine laughter at that sweet pair. I found something which was written on another subject but somehow seems to have been written for them:

"What else had they been born for—it was their chance. With gay hearts, they gave their greatest gift and with a smile to think that after all they had something to give which was of value. One by one death challenged them; one by one, they smiled in his grim visage and refused to be dismayed. They had found the path that led them home and when at last they laid their lives at the feet of the Good Shepherd, what could he do, but smile."

A number of years ago I found a poem that I liked very much and after I got to know Stan, I sent it to him a couple of Christmases ago as a Christmas card, and he called me and said how much he loved it and he was going to keep it. It's called "A Prayer for Clowns."

God bless all clowns
Who star the world with laughter
Who ring the rafters with a flying jest,
Who make the world spin merry on its way
And somehow add more beauty to each day.

God bless all clowns
So poor the world would be
Lacking their piquant touch, hilarity,
The belly laughs, the ringing lovely mirth
That makes a friendly place of this earth.

God bless all clowns—
Give them a long good life.
Make bright their way—they're a race apart!
Alchemists most, who turn their hearts' pain
Into a dazzling jest to lift the heart.

God bless all clowns.

I'd just like to say to Stan what he always said to all of us when we took his leave: God bless.

Irving Paul Lazar

March 28, 1907 ~ December 30, 1993

Tribute delivered by Larry McMurtry
at a memorial service

Irving Paul Lazar

The literary and entertainment agent Irving Paul (Swifty) Lazar was born in Brooklyn, New York, the son of Samuel Mortimer and Stari (DeLongpré) Lazar. A student at Fordham University in 1926, he was awarded a bachelor's of law from Brooklyn Law School in 1931. After graduation, he joined a New York City law firm, working with clients in show business. In 1936 he joined the Music Corporation of America, and began receiving an agent's 10 percent commission instead of a lawyer's 1 percent. During World War II he served in the U.S. Air Force, where he was instrumental in bringing about the service's film *Winged Victory*. He attained the rank of captain as well as an important client, Moss Hart, who had done much of the writing for the film.

Following the war, Lazar was an artists' representative for writers and directors from Hollywood to Broadway. His clients included such personalities as Ira Gershwin, Cole Porter, Ernest Hemingway, John Huston, and Neil Simon. Famous for his record-breaking deals, he often sold properties before they were produced. Lazar was also known for his pre-Oscar galas in Los Angeles, attended by stars and celebrities.

Larry McMurtry

The author Larry Jeff McMurtry was born in Wichita Falls, Texas, on June 3, 1936, the son of William Jefferson and Hazel Ruth (McIver) McMurtry. He married Josephine Ballard in 1959. The couple had one child and were divorced in 1966.

McMurtry received a B.A. from North Texas State College in 1958, and an M.A. from Rice University in 1960.

McMurtry is a prolific author of such novels as *The Last Picture Show* (1966), *Terms of Endearment* (1975), *Cadillac Jack* (1982), and the

1986 Pulitzer Prize–winning *Lonesome Dove* (1985). An accomplished screenwriter as well, McMurtry coauthored (with Peter Bogdanovich) the screenplay of *The Last Picture Show,* which was nominated for a 1971 Academy Award for best adapted screenplay.

McMurtry became a Wallace Stegner fellow in 1960, and a Guggenheim fellow in 1964. In 1986 he was the recipient of the Barbara McCombs/Lon Tinkle award of the Texas Institute of Letters. He is a member of the Texas Institute of Letters, which awarded him its Jesse H. Jones award in 1962.

Mr. McMurtry was a longtime client and close friend of Mr. Lazar.

Tribute for Irving Paul Lazar by Larry McMurtry

The first reference I can remember seeing to Irving Paul Lazar was in S. J. Perelman's *Paris Review* interview. Mr. Perelman, himself a notably stylish and fastidious traveler—I believe he drove a Mercedes along the Silk Road as far as Tashkent—mentioned in passing that the only man he knew who could step off an airplane anywhere in the world with his hands in his pockets was Irving Lazar.

I was a youth when I read that passage, and did not understand what a resonant tribute it was: a compliment paid by one great stylist to another. As a wordsmith S. J. Perelman was impeccable; as a traveler, like most of us but unlike Irving, he tended to get frazzled.

Irving Lazar's style, at home or abroad, did not tolerate frazzlement. He stepped off the plane with his hands in his pockets—excellently turned pockets, too—minus such impediments as the suit bags, claim checks, diaper bags, crumpled tickets, and lost composure that burden most mortals when they travel.

A mere six weeks before Irving's death I dined with him at Chasen's. He was in a wheelchair then. When we returned home he wheeled himself around his house for a while, looking for some object or other to give me; while he wandered and considered, remembering the shop off Bond Street where he picked up his bone china, or the gallery in Nice where he secured the little Matisse, I happened to open a silver cigarette box given him by Walter and Carol Matthau. It was engraved with the following tribute: "You have that rarest of things, an evolved heart."

Well, so he did—and he had an evolved style, too. But there is a catch-22 to great styles: the higher you wind them, the tighter the catch. Our styles tend to make us; then, if we last long enough and nothing beats them to it, they break us. Irving's devotion to fine European footwear rotted his feet and contributed its jot to his demise; but then, we are all going to demise some way. Who's to say that too-tight English shoes shouldn't introduce the finale?

When I read the Perelman interview I had no suspicion that the man named Irving Lazar, who stepped off planes on the preferable continents with his hands in his pockets, would someday be my agent. At the time, and for many years afterward, I had an agent, Dorothea Oppenheimer, a wonderful if eccentric woman who got through life on an intricate balance of beauty and bravura. Dorothea was born in a castle on the Danube and died in a one-room apartment on York Avenue, in New York City. In the three painful years that it took her to die, Irving, with uncustomary discretion, quietly did the work of agenting me. He treated Dorothea with the distinguished courtesy he bestowed on those who possessed what he called quality.

Dorothea Oppenheimer had quality, even in the dusty apartment on York Avenue, and unto the hour of her death. Irving deferred to it, and behaved impeccably. A dying, impoverished European woman got the credit—then minimal—for selling *Lonesome Dove.*

A few years later, Irving's eye for quality instantly spotted this elusive element in the appearance and demeanor of a much younger woman—my goddaughter Sara Ossana, then twelve. Irving and Mary were in London, ensconced in their accustomed suite at Claridge's, a suite the King of Spain was allowed to use when Irving didn't happen to be in town. Sara and her mother, Diana Ossana, now my screenwriting partner, happened to pass through on short notice; on even shorter notice (an hour, approximately), I called Irving and suggested dinner. The Lazars had planned to go to a birthday party to which numerous Windsors were coming, including the Queen and the glamorous young Princess of Wales.

Irving instantly changed his plans. "I see those people all the time," he said, and an hour later Sara and Diana and I were dining with Irving and Mary in the grand ballroom of Claridge's. Irving spent the evening admiring Sara's haircut—a world-class haircut she had given herself, only the day before—and harassing the captain to rush ever more delicacies to Sara's plate. On the basis of an excellent haircut and a few minutes conversation, Irving took Sara up and was unfailingly generous to her from then on. She was one of the few young women of her generation allowed to bring her boyfriend to the Oscar party; to the end, Sara loved Irving and Irving, Sara.

T. S. Eliot once made a famous remark about Henry James, who, Eliot said, had a mind so fine that no idea could penetrate it. Irving's mind was not unlike Henry James's. The texts that he agented rarely, if ever, penetrated it, except by osmosis. For years, once he became my agent, I waited for some chance statement that would indicate that he had read at least a page or two of the many books he agented for me; the statement never came.

Life, in the Scott Fitzgerald sense, was always glimmering out there somewhere; drinks, fine women, dancing, French food, exciting talk, and the endless parade of the great and famous, the beautiful and bold, were Irving's texts. Not for him the contemplative hour with Horace or Virgil; despite which he was, in his bones, a literary man. He honored writers and never, to my knowledge, allowed himself to confuse the work of literature with the subliterary best-seller. He reaped millions off best-sellers—in the way of the street—but his first and fiercest loyalties were to those who attempted literature, and, Truman Capote excepted, he didn't expect to find them at Spago or Le Cirque.

As a man of the cafe and the boulevard, Irving lavished his energies on not a few people who were spoiled well past the point of putrification; he was sometimes careless when it came to separating the wheat from the chaff. But manners—what he called "the correct thing"—mattered to him to the end. If Irving really cared about you, as he cared, for example, for Dorothea and Sara, it was necessary that you do the correct thing. With Dorothea this meant dying with her courage intact. With Sara, it meant exacting discipline in the matter of haircuts. When people abandoned their standards, and proved unable, in the difficult situation that life is sure to bring us, to do the correct thing, Irving's judgment was immediate and, frequently, final. Lady Keith could tell you.

In his year of bereavement, after Mary's death, Diana and Sara and I saw Irving often. On our last visit, a few weeks ago, he rose out of sedation and talked lucidly and lovingly, for almost an hour, about Bogart and Hemingway. He spoke about Bogart's death, and Hemingway's torment. But then he began to reminisce about their good times—he ceased to talk about them as if they were dead and spoke as he might speak of people who were traveling, people whom he would probably see again, as it might be, when he was passing through Paris, or lunching at "21."

In humans the grace that lasts is probably always moral, and always tragic. Irving and Mary are gone, and the community of the arts is diminished. Irving was a larger-than-life figure in a town that, but for the great magnifying glass of the screen, would be in most ways smaller than life. His intelligence and his taste brought an element of refinement to a culture in most ways crude. His taste reached back to the Europe of the great West Coast emigrés: Mann, Stravinsky, Renoir.

There are few links to that time left, and none who sustained the range of contact and reference that Irving Lazar commanded. With his passing, in the words of Thomas Nashe, the Renaissance poet, a brightness has fallen from the air. Irving himself, at his eighty-fifth birthday party, lamented the devaluation of glamour, as he saw it, in a town where movie stars seldom take the trouble to be movie stars anymore.

Once, speaking of President Reagan, whose memoirs he didn't get to agent, Irving consoled himself with this reflection: "That's all right—pretty soon he'll be where Franco is."

As it happened, Irving took ship first. The prince of agents, the man who could step ashore, or out of a plane, or off a train with his hands in his pockets, is traveling now. We can be sure that a car will be waiting, at the dock, or the airport, or the station. The best suite will be his, and the best hotel; the clothes will have been unpacked; the captain will be waiting deferentially at the best table in the best restaurant, where the best company will soon gather to dine and drink till eternity cracks.

He won't be sitting with Franco, though. Irving will be traveling in that greatly peopled bourne where Mr. Kafka dines with Mr. Woolf and Papa breaks bread with Beaudelaire. And should it be that either the Lord of Light or (better yet) the Prince of Darkness is ready to sell his memoirs, Irving Paul Lazar will get right on the phone.

Mickey Mantle

October 20, 1931 ~ August 13, 1995

Eulogy delivered by Bob Costas at the funeral,
Dallas, Texas, August 15, 1995

Mickey Mantle

American baseball player Mickey Charles Mantle was born in Spavinaw, Oklahoma. The son of Elvin Clark and Lovell (Richardson) Mantle, he married Merlyn Louise Johnson in 1951, and together they had four children.

Mantle began his baseball career as a shortstop in the minor leagues, and switched to right field when he joined the Yankees in 1951. When Joe DiMaggio retired in 1952, Mantle moved to center field—the position he played for almost his entire career. Mantle was the most powerful switch-hitter in baseball history: 536 home runs, 1,509 runs batted in, and a career batting average of .298. He won baseball's Triple Crown in 1956 with a .352 batting average, 52 home runs, and 130 runs batted in.

Mantle retired in 1969 and, as with other Yankee greats Babe Ruth, Lou Gehrig, and Joe DiMaggio, his uniform number was retired as well. In 1974 he was inducted into the Baseball Hall of Fame in Cooperstown, New York. He died in Dallas, Texas, where he made his home.

Bob Costas

Sports announcer Bob Costas is a native of Queens, New York, and attended Syracuse University, where he majored in journalism. He began his professional career at Syracuse's WSYR-TV and Radio in 1973 while studying at the university.

In 1974, he began at KMOX Radio in St. Louis, Missouri, one of America's most prominent radio stations, broadcasting a wide variety of live, play-by-play, and studio programs until 1981. During this time he did regional NFL and NBA telecasts for CBS (1976 to 1979) and the NBA's Chicago Bulls (1980).

Costas began his career at NBC Sports in 1980 as a football and basketball play-by-play man. From 1983 through 1990, he teamed with analyst Tony Kubek on NBC's "Game of the Week" baseball telecasts, and hosted the network's "NFL Live" pregame show from 1984 to 1992. He has anchored the network's coverage of the last two summer Olym-pics, winning an Emmy for his coverage of the 1992 games in Barcelona, Spain.

In 1988, Costas began to diversify beyond sports broadcasting, serving as a substitute host for Bryant Gumbel on NBC's *Today Show* and as host for his own late-night program, *Later . . . with Bob Costas,* until 1994. Costas now holds a unique position with NBC, contributing to the network in sports, news, and entertainment. He is the host of the network's acclaimed coverage of the NBA, and the play-by-play announcer for its major league baseball telecasts. A regular contributor to NBC news, Costas provides reports and interviews for the network's prime-time news magazines. He has won the Emmy award for outstanding sports broadcaster six times, and has been named by his peers as the National Sportscaster of the Year five times.

Bob Costas resides in St. Louis, Missouri, with his wife, Randy, and their two children, and was a longtime friend and admirer of Mickey Mantle.

Eulogy for Mickey Mantle by Bob Costas

You know, it occurs to me as we're all sitting here thinking of Mickey, he's probably somewhere getting an earful from Casey Stengel, and no doubt quite confused by now.

One of Mickey's fondest wishes was that he be remembered as a great teammate, to know that the men he played with thought well of him.

But it was more than that. Moose and Whitey and Tony and Yogi and Bobby and Hank, what a remarkable team you were. And the stories of the visits you guys made to Mickey's bedside the last few days were heartbreakingly tender. It meant everything to Mickey, as would the presence of so many baseball figures past and present here today.

I was honored to be asked to speak by the Mantle family today. I am not standing here as a broadcaster. Mel Allen is the eternal voice of the Yankees and that would be his place. And there are others here with a longer and deeper association with Mickey than mine.

But I guess I'm here, not so much to speak for myself, as to simply represent the millions of baseball-loving kids who grew up in the fifties and sixties and for whom Mickey Mantle was baseball.

And more than that, he was a presence in our lives—a fragile hero to whom we had an emotional attachment so strong and lasting that it defied logic. Mickey often said he didn't understand it, this enduring connection and affection—the men now in their forties and fifties, otherwise perfectly sensible, who went dry in the mouth and stammered like schoolboys in the presence of Mickey Mantle.

Maybe Mickey was uncomfortable with it, not just because of his basic shyness, but because he was always too honest to regard himself as some kind of deity.

But that was never really the point. In a very different time than today, the first baseball commissioner, Kenesaw Mountain Landis, said, "Every boy builds a shrine to some baseball hero, and before that shrine, a candle always burns."

For a huge portion of my generation, Mickey Mantle was that baseball hero. And for reasons that no statistics, no dry recitation of facts can possibly capture, he was the most compelling baseball hero of our lifetime. And he was our symbol of baseball at a time when the game meant something to us that perhaps it no longer does.

Mickey Mantle had those dual qualities so seldom seen—exuding dynamism and excitement, but at the same time touching your heart—flawed, wounded. We knew there was something poignant about Mickey Mantle before we knew what poignant meant. We didn't just root for him, we felt for him.

Long before many of us ever cracked a serious book, we knew something about mythology as we watched Mickey Mantle run out a home run through the lengthening shadows of a late Sunday afternoon at Yankee Stadium.

There was greatness in him, but vulnerability, too.

He was our guy. When he was hot, we felt great. When he slumped or got hurt, we sagged a bit, too. We tried to crease our caps like him; kneel in an imaginary on-deck circle like him; run like him, heads down, elbows up.

Billy Crystal is here today. Billy says that at his bar mitzvah he spoke in an Oklahoma drawl. Billy's here today because he loved Mickey Mantle, and millions more who felt like him are here today in spirit as well.

It has been said that the truth is never pure and rarely simple.

Mickey Mantle was too humble and honest to believe that the whole truth about him could be found on a Wheaties box or a baseball card. But the emotional truths of childhood have a power that transcends objective fact. They stay with us through all the years, withstanding the ambivalence that so often accompanies the experience of adults.

That's why we can still recall the immediate tingle in that instant of recognition when a Mickey Mantle popped up in a pack of Topps bubble gum cards—a treasure lodged between an Eli Grba and a Pumpsie Green.

That's why we smile today, recalling those October afternoons when we'd sneak a transistor radio into school to follow Mickey and the Yankees in the World Series.

Or when I think of Mr. Tomasi, a very wise sixth-grade teacher who understood that the World Series was more important, at least for one day, than any school lesson could be. So he brought his black-and-white TV from home, plugged it in and let us watch it right there in school through the flicker and the static. It was richer and more compelling than anything I've seen on a high-resolution, big-screen TV.

Of course, the bad part, Bobby, was that Koufax struck fifteen of you guys out that day.

My phone's been ringing the past few weeks as Mickey fought for his life. I've heard from people I hadn't seen or talked to in years—guys I played stickball with, even some guys who took Willie's side in those endless Mantle-Mays arguments. They're grown up now. They have their families. They're not even necessarily big baseball fans anymore. But they felt something hearing about Mickey, and they figured I did, too.

In the last year, Mickey Mantle, always so hard on himself, finally came to accept and appreciate that distinction between a role model and a hero. The first he often was not, the second he always will be.

And, in the end, people got it. And Mickey Mantle got from America something other than misplaced and mindless celebrity worship. He got something far more meaningful. He got love—love for what he had been, love for what he made us feel, love for the humanity and sweetness that was always there mixed in with the flaws and all the pain that wracked his body and his soul.

We wanted to tell him that it was OK, that what he had been was enough. We hoped he felt that Mutt Mantle would have understood and that Merlyn and the boys loved him.

And then in the end, something remarkable happened—the way it does for champions. Mickey Mantle rallied. His heart took over, and he had some innings as fine as any in 1956 or with his buddy, Roger, in 1961.

But this time, he did it in the harsh and trying summer of '95. And what he did was stunning. The sheer grace of that ninth inning—the humility, the sense of humor, the total absence of self-pity, the simple eloquence and honesty of his pleas to others to take heed of his mistakes.

All of America watched in admiration. His doctors said he was, in many ways, the most remarkable patient they'd ever seen. His bravery, so stark and real, that even those used to seeing people in dire circumstances were moved by his example.

Because of that example, organ donations are up dramatically all across America. A cautionary tale has been honestly told and perhaps will affect some lives for the better.

And our last memories of Mickey Mantle are as heroic as the first.

None of us, Mickey included, would want to be held to account for every moment of our lives. But how many of us could say that our best moments were as magnificent as his?

This is the cartoon from this morning's *Dallas Morning News.* Maybe some of you saw it. It got torn a little bit on the way from the hotel to here. There's a figure here, St. Peter I take it to be, with his arm around Mickey, that broad back and the number seven. He's holding his book of admissions. He says "Kid, that was the most courageous ninth inning I've ever seen."

It brings to mind a story Mickey liked to tell on himself and maybe some of you have heard it. He pictured himself at the pearly gates, met by St. Peter, who shook his head and said, "Mick, we checked the record. We know some of what went on. Sorry, we can't let you in, but before you go, God wants to know if you'd sign these six dozen baseballs."

Well, there were days when Mickey Mantle was so darn good that we kids would bet that even God would want his autograph. But like the cartoon says, I don't think Mick needed to worry much about the other part.

I just hope God has a place for him where he can run again. Where he can play practical jokes on his teammates and smile that boyish smile, 'cause God knows, no one's perfect. And God knows there's something special about heroes.

So long, Mick. Thanks.

George C. Marshall

December 31, 1880 ~ October 16, 1959

Eulogy delivered by Frank McCarthy
at a memorial service, Virginia Military Institute,
Lexington, Virginia, October 21, 1959

George C. Marshall

American soldier and statesman George Catlett Marshall Jr. was born in Uniontown, Pennsylvania. He was educated at the Virginia Military Institute, and received his Army commission in 1902. In a series of appointments prior to the outbreak of World War I, Marshall proved himself to be an outstanding staff officer. Possessed of a powerful memory, he provided quick insight into tactical problems. After the United States entered World War I in 1917, he was sent to France as assistant chief of staff of the First Division. There, he caught the attention of General John Pershing and served as his principal aide until 1924.

During the twenties and thirties, Marshall continued his steady rise in rank, building upon his reputation as a first-rate administrator. In 1939, on the verge of World War II, he became chief of staff and directed the United States Army throughout World War II.

Marshall spent the next two years in China as special representative of the president, trying to negotiate a coalition government. He became secretary of state in 1947, and originated the Marshall Plan for the postwar reconstruction of Europe. He resigned the position in 1949 because of poor health, and after a lengthy rest was appointed secretary of defense in 1950, at the onset of the Korean War.

Marshall was awarded the Nobel Peace Prize in 1953 for his contributions to the postwar world—the only professional soldier to receive the honor.

Frank McCarthy

Film producer and retired brigadier general Frank McCarthy was born in Richmond, Virginia, on June 8, 1912, the son of Frank J. and Lillian

(Binford) McCarthy. He was granted an A.B. from the Virginia Military Institute in 1933, and an A.M. from the University of Virginia in 1940. From 1935 to 1936, he was a reporter for the *Richmond* (Va.) *News Leader,* and from 1937 to 1939 he was the press agent for the New York theatrical producer George Abbott.

From 1941 to 1943, McCarthy was the military secretary to the chief of staff of the War Department. In 1944, he was appointed the assistant secretary of the War Department's general staff, and served General George Marshall in that capacity until 1945. During World War II he was decorated with the Distinguished Service Medal and the Legion of Merit, and was named an Officer of the Most Excellent Order of the British Empire. In 1945 he served as the assistant secretary of state, and spent the next three years in Europe as the representative of the Motion Picture Association of America.

McCarthy was an executive and producer at 20th Century-Fox Studios from 1949 to 1962, and from 1965 to 1972. He also produced films for Universal Studios from 1963 to 1965, and from 1972 to 1977. The films he produced during that time include *Decision before Dawn, Sailor of the King, A Guide for the Married Man,* and *MacArthur*. His production of *Patton* won seven Academy Awards, including the best picture in 1970.

McCarthy was named Virginian of the Year by the Virginian Press Association in 1970. He was a member of the Academy of Motion Picture Arts and Sciences, and a trustee of the George C. Marshall Research Foundation.

Frank McCarthy died on December 1, 1986, in Los Angeles. He served with General Marshall and was a close friend.

Eulogy for George C. Marshall by Frank McCarthy

Yesterday afternoon in Arlington National Cemetery, on a gentle hillside overlooking Washington and the Potomac, a group of old friends gathered at a graveside to say farewell to General of the Army George Catlett Marshall. One might have supposed that this company would consist of cabinet officers, ambassadors, generals, and admirals. There were, indeed, a few men of fame and position, but only those few who had made impressions upon General Marshall through congeniality and affection, rather than through rank or station. The others present ranged from associates of his school days, his early service in China and the Philippines, and his retirement at Leesburg, to his orderly and his old driver.

The character of this assemblage reminded me once again of the simplicity and sincerity of this great man, which stood in sharp contrast to what the record shows of his high achievements.

Even before the First World War, when General Marshall was a first lieutenant, General Franklin Bell described him as "the greatest military genius in America since Stonewall Jackson," and added, "Keep your eye on George Marshall."

After the First World War General Pershing, on whose staff General Marshall had served as a colonel, referred to him as the finest officer produced by that conflict.

During the Second World War, when Prime Minister Churchill proposed General Marshall for command of the Allied Expeditionary Force, President Roosevelt said, "I could not sleep with General Marshall out of the country." He recognized that, important though the war with Germany was, we were engaged in a global war, with a Washington command post which must be directed by the finest military mind in the free world.

After the Second World War, President Truman expressed the opinion that this conflict could not have been won without General Marshall's leadership. In later years he referred to the General as "the greatest living American." In characterizing him thus, Mr. Truman saluted General Marshall's achievements, not only as chief of staff of the Army, but also as secretary of state and secretary of defense. In the former office, the General devised the plan which bore his name, and without which Western Europe would most certainly have moved into the Communist orbit before 1950, through use of the ballot and without bloodshed. As secretary of defense, he restored to our depleted armed forces the military posture which has made them capable of deterring war in all the years that have followed.

In contrast, once more, to this impressive record, I should like to give you a few anecdotes, some of them rather personal in nature, which demonstrate General Marshall's basic virtues:

He was devoted to duty. When he proposed a course of action to a superior and it was adopted, he declined to accept credit if it was successful, but insisted upon accepting blame if it failed. When General Patton was under attack by the entire press of the world for taking physical action against a malingering soldier, General Marshall sent General Eisenhower the most remarkable message I have ever read. It said, "If you consider that General Patton's value as a commander outweighs the damage which he has done to his prestige and that of the Army, keep him. If not, General Patton should be relieved. But do not relieve him yourself; let me do that. Your burden in the conduct of battle is so great that I can better bear the pain of removing this fine officer, if you consider it necessary." I would like to remind you that General Patton was the only senior officer in the Army whom I ever heard General Marshall call by his first name.

General Marshall was selfless. When I became the secretary of his staff, he advised me that, if anyone should give him a medal, confer an honorary degree upon him, or write a book about him during my incumbency, I would be immediately relieved. Other secretaries of the General's staff received identical instructions. When offered large sums for his memoirs, General Marshall invariably replied that he was admitted to the councils of the president, the prime minister, and the great military staffs as a confidential conferee, not as a reporter for the *Saturday Evening Post.*

General Marshall was a man of judgment. He told me once that a good officer obeyed regulations, but that a superior officer recognized the point at which they become inapplicable and threw them away.

General Marshall was a simple man. At the coronation of Queen Elizabeth, the entire audience arose in respect as he and Mrs. Marshall walked up the aisle to the front of the Westminster Abbey. Turning to enter his pew, he glanced behind him to see what person of note had commanded this tribute.

General Marshall was a man of humor. Once on an inspection tour in New Guinea, he released me to attend a picnic with a group of officers and nurses. We became lost in the jungle during a severe tropical storm, and all of us suffered from exposure and exhaustion. As I was taken into General Marshall's plane on a stretcher, another officer expressed sympathy at my condition. "Don't trouble about him," said General Marshall. "He's the only one who has had any romance on this trip."

In that simple service yesterday, Chaplain Luther Miller said, "O, Eternal God, suffer us not to miss the glory of this hour."

He referred of course, to the glory of the life which General Marshall had led, and to our gratitude to God that this great man walked among us. We VMI cadets and alumni have a special cause for gratitude, which is best summed up, I think, in the words of President Eisenhower: "Any school that can boast graduates like General Marshall, and all his associates who have been so valuable in wartime and peacetime service to this country, is indeed a distinguished institution and one that we certainly will nourish as long as there is an America."

If I should be asked for the few lines that best characterize the most distinguished graduate in VMI's 120 years of history, I should quote the lines engraved at the base of our own Sir Moses Ezekiel's statue to the Confederate soldier in Arlington:

Not for fame or reward
Not for place or rank
Not lured by ambition
Nor goaded by necessity
But in simple obedience to duty as he understood it
This man suffered all
sacrificed all
dared all
and died.

Thurgood Marshall

July 2, 1908 ~ January 24, 1993

Eulogy delivered by Chief Justice William H. Rehnquist, Washington Cathedral, Washington, D.C., January 28, 1993

Thurgood Marshall

Supreme Court justice and civil rights advocate Thurgood Marshall was born in Baltimore, the son of William and Norma (Williams) Marshall. In 1929, he married Vivian Burey; he later married Cecilia S. Suyat in 1955. Marshall was the father of two children. He received a bachelor of arts degree from Lincoln University in 1930, and was the class of 1933's valedictorian from Howard University Law School.

Marshall practiced law in Baltimore from 1933 to 1937, and in 1938 became national counsel for the NAACP. The following year he helped found the organization's Legal Defense and Educational Fund, whose purpose was to legally challenge segregation. During this time, he won twenty-nine out of the thirty-two cases he argued, the most famous being the 1954 landmark, *Brown v. Board of Education,* which struck down segregation in the nation's public schools.

He was appointed U.S. circuit judge for the federal appeals circuit in 1961, and was solicitor general of the United States from 1965 to 1967.

President Lyndon Johnson appointed Marshall a U.S. Supreme Court justice in 1967, the first African American to hold the office. A consistent liberal, Marshall found himself increasingly in the minority as the makeup of the Court evolved.

Marshall retired in 1991 due to ill health, and his seat was occupied by Clarence Thomas.

William H. Rehnquist

United States Supreme Court justice William Hubbs Rehnquist was born in Milwaukee on October 1, 1924, the son of William Benjamin and Margery (Peck) Rehnquist. Rehnquist married Natalie Cornell in 1953, and the couple have three children. Earning a B.A. from Stanford University in 1948, Rehnquist was awarded an M.A. from Harvard in 1949. He returned to Stanford, where in 1952 he received an LL.B.

Rehnquist was law clerk to former U.S. Supreme Court justice Robert H. Jackson from 1952 to 1953, and for the next fifteen years was associated with different Phoenix law firms, including a partnership in the firm Powers & Rehnquist from 1960 to 1969.

From 1969 to 1971, Rehnquist served as the assistant attorney general and legal counsel during the Nixon administration, where he promoted an anticrime stance and opposed civil rights measures. Despite liberal opposition, Nixon appointed him an associate justice of the Supreme Court in 1971, in which position he served until 1986. In that year, President Ronald Reagan named him chief justice of the Supreme Court. Justice Rehnquist served with Justice Marshall on the Supreme Court for twenty years.

Eulogy for Thurgood Marshall by William H. Rehnquist

Thurgood Marshall was an extraordinary man. He served for twenty-four years as a justice of the Supreme Court of the United States. Yet before he ever took his seat on that Court, he had designed and carried out a legal strategy which resulted in the overturning of laws which discriminated by race in schools, transportation, housing, and the voting booth. Under his leadership, the American constitutional landscape in the area of equal protection of the laws was rewritten.

The list of cases that he argued and won before the Supreme Court of the United States is a long one. The names and holdings of the leading cases are known to every practitioner and student of constitutional law. *Smith v. Allwright, Shelley v. Kraemer, Sweatt v. Painter,* and finally, his greatest victory, the landmark case of *Brown v. Board of Education.*

His remarkable accomplishments as a private lawyer were followed by appointment to the Court of Appeals for the Second Circuit, as solicitor general, and finally as an associate justice of the Supreme Court. In these quite different roles, his contributions to public law were necessarily of a different kind. On the Supreme Court, he continued to be a vigorous champion of civil rights for minorities and civil liberty for all; sometimes in the majority, just as often in dissent. But he authored important opinions in areas of the law quite apart from those with which he is usually associated. His opinions for the Court, for example, in *Loretto v. Teleprompter* and *FCC v. Florida Power Company,* remain important landmarks in the interpretation of the Takings Clause of the Fifth Amendment. During his twenty-four years as a member of the Court, he wrote more than three hundred majority opinions.

We who sat with him during this time learned to value his wise counsel in conference. We also looked forward to those occasions on which he would recount some of his experiences as a civil rights lawyer in often bitterly hostile towns and distinctly unfriendly courtrooms. Many of these stories had a humorous twist to them, but they also gave us a sense of what he had been up against in many of his cases. His forays to represent his clients required not only diligence and legal skill, but physical courage of a high order. When I read today of highly paid young lawyers in large law firms complaining about how dull the life of a corporate lawyer is, I cannot help but contrast them with the career of Thurgood Marshall as a practicing lawyer—not as rewarding financially to be sure, but so much more rewarding professionally and personally.

As a result of his career as a lawyer and judge, Thurgood Marshall left an indelible mark not just upon the law but upon his country. Inscribed above the front entrance to the Supreme Court building are the words "Equal Justice Under Law." Surely no one individual did more to make these words a reality than Thurgood Marshall.

Gerry Mulligan

April 6, 1927 ~ January 20, 1996

Tribute, "In Memory, A Personal Remembrance," by Dave Brubeck, *DBQ Newsletter*

Gerry Mulligan

Jazz musician, composer, and arranger Gerald Joseph Mulligan was born in New York City, the son of George V. R. and Louise (Shannon) Mulligan. He married Contessa Franca Rota, with whom he had one son. As a child, Mulligan learned to play first the piano, then wind instruments. By high school, he was a professional arranger, and dropped out of school to work with big bands. Mulligan studied with many notable musicians, including Sam Correnti (who taught him saxophone), Johnny Warrington, Gil Evans, Charlie Parker, and Duke Ellington (who taught him arranging and composition). Working with Miles Davis, he was a major contributor to the development of the "cool" school of jazz.

He was the leader of the Gerry Mulligan Quartet from 1951 to 1956, and toured Europe and Japan with his thirteen-piece band in the early sixties. Upon his return to the United States, he worked with various musicians, most notably as sideman with Dave Brubeck. Mulligan toured extensively throughout the seventies and eighties with his own bands, and recorded with such artists as Paul Desmond, Thelonious Monk, and Stan Getz. His albums include *Birth of the Cool, The Age of Steam,* and *Walk on Water,* which won a Grammy award in 1981.

Mulligan is recognized as one of the best jazz baritone saxophonists of all time, and has received numerous awards. He was made a Duke Ellington fellow of Yale University, and in 1993 was named to the *Down Beat* Hall of Fame.

Dave Brubeck

Jazz musician David Warren Brubeck was born in Concord, California, on December 6, 1920, the son of Howard and Elizabeth (Ivey) Brubeck. He married Iola Whitlock in 1942, and the couple have six children.

Brubeck earned a B.A. from The University of the Pacific in 1942, and did postgraduate study with Darius Milhaud at Mills College from 1946 to 1949.

Beginning in 1946, he was the leader of several musical ensembles, and formed the Dave Brubeck Quartet in 1951, playing at colleges, festivals, clubs, and with symphony orchestras. His discography includes recordings with Columbia, Decca, Telare, and Time Out. His recording with the latter company was the first jazz album to receive a gold record.

Brubeck's compositions include the ballets *Points on Jazz* and *Glances,* large orchestral works, oratorios, cantatas, and piano works, as well as over one hundred jazz compositions, including *Blue Rondo a la Turk, In Your Own Sweet Way,* and *The Duke*.

From 1952 to 1955, Brubeck was the winner of several jazz polls conducted by such magazines as *Downbeat, Billboard,* and *Playboy,* and in 1954 he became the first jazz musician to appear on the cover of *Time*. Brubeck received the B.M.I. Jazz Pioneer award in 1985, and was inducted into the Hollywood Walk of Fame in 1992. Brubeck received a National Medal of the Arts in 1994 and became a member of the American Jazz Hall of Fame in 1995, winning a Lifetime Achievement award from the NARAS in 1996. He is also a Duke Ellington fellow of Yale University.

Dave Brubeck and Gerry Mulligan were friends for over forty years, and appeared and toured together on numerous occasions.

Tribute for Gerry Mulligan by Dave Brubeck

It is difficult for me to realize that it was only a year ago at this time that we toured Europe together. Our group would open the show, and after our bows, Gerry and I would return to the stage alone. Each night as we swung into "These Foolish Things" the mood would be different—sometimes lyrical and sad, sometimes hard and swinging, sometimes with gentle humor—but never, never a repeated formula. That was the genius of Gerry Mulligan.

Our careers first intersected in California in the early '50s. Gerry had already gained a reputation for his work with Gene Krupa, Claude Thornhill, Elliot Lawrence, and "Birth of the Cool" when he decided to come West. At that time I was just starting Fantasy Records with the Weiss brothers and recommended to them that they record the fantastic young group from Los Angeles which consisted of Gerry Mulligan, Chet Baker, Carson Smith, and Chico Hamilton. They were playing occasionally at The Haig in Los Angeles, a tiny club that featured modern jazz. I talked the Blackhawk owners into making a swap. They bring Gerry up to San Francisco and I would go to The Haig, thereby helping both of us reach a larger audience, and hopefully to sell more records. Gerry used to say that I got him his first "steady gig."

During the '50s our paths crossed often. We toured together in a package show that consisted of Duke Ellington and his Orchestra, Stan Getz's group, Gerry's group, and mine. Of course, Gerry was a regular at the Newport Jazz Festivals and all the other jazz events as the festival concept spread to other cities and to Europe. He was known for his eagerness to "sit in" with any group, any style, any vintage. Any group he organized, big band or small, had his individual, innovative stamp.

In the '60s, after I had moved to Connecticut and Gerry, too, was back on the East Coast, he would occasionally "sub" for Desmond, if Paul could not make a gig. And sometimes both Gerry and Paul would tour with me and my rhythm section. In 1968, a few months after I disbanded the quartet, festival organizer George Wein approached me about returning to Mexico. I told him I no longer had a group. Wein responded that he had already hired Gerry Mulligan as a soloist, would I consider finding a rhythm section and playing with him? It seemed a natural move, but where could I find a rhythm section of the same caliber as Joe Morello and Eugene Wright? Joyce (Mrs. George Wein) suggested Boston-based drummer Alan Dawson; and I had already been impressed with the work of bassist Jack Six, who had stepped in at the last minute to play my oratorio "The Light in the Wilderness." What began as a temporary band became a fixture on the jazz scene throughout the '70s (and Jack Six is still playing bass with me).

From 1968 to 1975 Gerry and I toured together in Australia, Japan, Mexico, and all of Europe, and crisscrossed the United States and Canada playing colleges, concert halls, and festivals. Gerry often joined "Two Generations of Brubeck" through the '70s, and wrote and rehearsed material with the Darius Brubeck Ensemble. He referred to himself as the guest who came to dinner and remained for almost ten years. We made only two studio recordings in that period, "Blues Roots" (Columbia) and "We're All Together Again for the First Time" (Atlantic), but live performances were recorded in Mexico ("Compadres" on that initial 1968 tour), "The Last Set at Newport" (Atlantic) and "Live at the Berlin Philharmonic" (CBS) in 1972. Also, during our time together Gerry played his first "gig" with a symphony orchestra. It was with Erich Kunzel and the Cincinnati Symphony (1970), and recorded by Decca (now reissued on MCA).

Gerry's musical gifts were so natural that once he made a decision to master something, he quickly set about learning and doing. The next thing I knew he was studying in Milan, Italy; then I learned he had a commission from Zubin Mehta to write a piece for the New York Philharmonic. A few years later I received from Gerry a gift of his orchestral recording "Symphonic Dreams," compositions by Gerry, performed by the Houston Symphony conducted by Erich Kunzel. In the liner notes he had highlighted my name among "those who helped give me confidence that I could do it."

For a number of years Gerry and I have lived not far from each other in Connecticut. But due to both our schedules, our visits in each other's homes were occasional but memorable. I smile to myself when I visualize him with my sons as he took over as chief session organizer at our fiftieth wedding anniversary party Iola and I gave after the Monterey Jazz Festival in 1992. He wrote a "wedding song" for us on that occasion and played with all the musicians, young and old.

In the last months of Gerry's life we visited by telephone before he left for each trip, and again upon his return. We talked to each other long distance when the family was gathering in London for my seventy-fifth birthday. He said, "I feel like I should be there, too." When we said "Goodbye" in late December, as he was making what was to be his final trip to Italy, we made a date to see each other after the first of the year when I got back from my Los Angeles concerts. My return was delayed by my own illness. We tried to call and missed each other. But through a mutual friend I heard he was improved. It was a false hope. The next phone call, when we arrived in Cincinnati on January 20, was to notify us of his death.

Franca, his wife, was composed and calm when we spoke to her. She told us that his passing was peaceful. I do believe he was prepared. Our mutual friend, Gene Lees, who writes *The Jazzletter,* spoke of Gerry's performances aboard the *SS Norway* cruise ship in November: "It was one of the finest and most inventive playing I ever heard from Gerry in the thirty-six years of our friendship. . . . I was in awe of what I heard. It had a compositional integrity beyond anything I ever heard in jazz. . . . It is not that his playing was abandoned, although it certainly was free. It was as if he had total control of it that he had been seeking all his life."

The people who gathered at his memorial service at St. Peter's in New York City paid him fitting tribute with music and words. It was a testimonial to his widespread interests because they were friends from all fields of music and from all periods of Gerry's life—songwriters, dramatists, band leaders, and, of course, many, many jazz musicians, David Amram, George Shearing, Art Farmer, Bill Crow, Phil Woods, to name just a few.

When I was called upon to speak, I remembered the conversation Gerry and I had when we recorded a duet last year for my new album. I started to play the old standard "Together" at a very slow tempo, in a rather sad and soulful way.

Gerry said, "How come you're playing it that way? It sounds so unhappy. Let's take it faster and brighter. Let me see the words." The words begin:

> "We strolled the lane, together,
> laughed at the rain, together."

"See," he said with triumph. "It's a happy song." But Gerry didn't read the final lines:

> "You're gone from me;
> but in my memory
> we will always be
> together."

At that point in my story I couldn't find my voice, so thinking of our duets, I played "These Foolish Things."

There were many great musical tributes by magnificent musicians. But the most extraordinary expression heard at the service came from Gerry himself, his last musical statement, recorded in his home shortly before his death.

> O Great Spirit
> whose voice I hear in the wind,
> whose breath gives light to the world,
> hear me;
> I am weak and small,
> I need your strength, your wisdom.
> May I walk in beauty,
> make my eyes behold the red and purple sunset,
> make my hands respect the things that you have made;
> make my ears shape to hear your voice,
> make me wise so that I may know the things you taught your children,
> the lessons you've written in ev'ry tree and rock;
> make me strong, not to be superior to my brothers,
> but to fight my greatest enemy, myself;
> make me ready to come to you with straight eyes,
> so when this life fades as the fading sunset
> my spirit may come to you without shame,
> without dishonor.

O Great Spirit
whose voice I hear in the wind;
whose breath gives light to the world,
hear me.
(Chief Yellow Lark's Prayer)

Edmund Muskie

March 28, 1914 ~ March 26, 1996

Eulogy delivered by President Jimmy Carter,
March 30, 1996

Edmund Muskie

Former senator and secretary of state Edmund Sixtus Muskie was born in Rumford, Maine, the son of Stephen and Josephine (Czarnecki) Muskie. He married Jane Frances Gray in 1948, and they had five children. In 1936, he graduated A.B. cum laude from Bates College; he received an LL.B. from Cornell in 1939, and served as a lieutenant in the United States Naval Reserve from 1942 to 1945.

Muskie began his career as a lawyer in Waterville, and was elected to the Maine House of Representatives in 1948, serving the Democratic floor leader from 1949 to 1951. He was a member of the Democratic National Committee from 1952 to 1955, and became governor of Maine in 1955, a position he held until 1959.

From 1959 to 1980 Muskie served as U.S. senator from Maine, adhering to the liberal Democratic agenda while proposing fiscal restraint. His most important contributions during his Senate years were in air and water pollution control, and solutions to urban problems. He served as chairman of the Budget Committee, chairman of the Governmental Affairs Committee, member of the Foreign Relations Committee, and assistant majority whip. In 1968, Muskie was the Democratic candidate for vice president, and in 1972 he was the victim of political "dirty tricks" during his run for the Democratic presidential nomination.

Muskie served as secretary of state under President Jimmy Carter from 1980 to 1981. He left the government in 1982 and was a partner in the Washington firm Chadbourne & Parke. He was a member of the Advisory Commission on Intergovernmental Relations, and the national executive director of AMVETS. He was the author of *Journeys* (1972), and with coauthor McGeorge Bundy wrote *Presidential Promises and Performances* (1980). In 1981, Muskie was the recipient of the Presidential Medal of Freedom and the Former Members of Congress Distinguished Service award.

Jimmy Carter

Former president of the United States James Earl (Jimmy) Carter Jr. was born in Plains, Georgia, on October 1, 1924, the son of James Earl and Lillian (Gordy) Carter. He married Rosalynn Smith in 1946, and the couple have four children. Carter was a student at Georgia Southwestern College from 1941 to 1942, and at the Georgia Institute of Technology from 1942 to 1943, graduating from the U.S. Naval Academy with a B.S. in 1946. Specializing in nuclear-powered submarines, he served as an engineer in the navy until his resignation in 1953.

A peanut farmer in his native Plains, Georgia, from 1953 to 1977, Carter served in the Georgia Senate from 1962 to 1966. He was the governor of Georgia from 1971 to 1975. In 1976, after running a campaign as the non-Washington politician, Carter was elected president of the United States. In domestic affairs, his policies concerning energy conservation, income tax, and welfare reform were stalled in Congress. While he did make some gains in foreign relations, these were overshadowed by the Iranian hostage crisis in 1980. He lost the 1980 presidential election to the Republican nominee, Ronald Reagan.

Carter has been a professor at Emory University in Atlanta since 1982, and has led international observer teams to Panama (1989) and Haiti (1990). He is the author of several books, including *Keeping Faith/Memoirs of a President* (1982), *Vision of the Next Generation* (1993), and *Always a Reckoning* (1995). Hailed for his humanitarian efforts, Carter has received numerous awards, including the Martin Luther King Jr. Nonviolent Peace Prize in 1979 and the Albert Schweitzer prize for humanitarianism in 1991.

Jimmy Carter and Edmund Muskie were longtime friends, and Muskie served as secretary of state in Carter's administration.

Eulogy for Edmund Muskie by Jimmy Carter

Ed Muskie had the appearance, the mannerisms, and the actions of a true statesman. I first came to know him when I became governor and faced almost overwhelming lobbying pressure from the power companies, with their smokestacks spewing forth black smoke, and the thirteen pulp mills in our state that were destroying our rivers.

I saw before me then the makings of an incredible political battle. But there was a hero in Washington who faced much greater lobbying pressure nationwide from the polluters of our streams and air. Ed

Muskie took them on, and he inspired me and many others to do the same.

In an unpublicized way, Ed Muskie also was a brave champion of basic civil rights at a time when it wasn't popular to be so. He worked hand in hand with Dr. Benjamin Mays, a hero of mine from Georgia, and inspired people like me and other public servants around the country, who looked on them both with great admiration.

And when he saw a budget problem in Washington, he decided to do something about it. He helped orchestrate and pass a new budget law. He became the first chairman of the Budget Committee. And despite formidable challenges that he faced then and that still trouble us today, he was able to bring order out of chaos and to work harmoniously not only with representatives, jealous of their own prerogatives, but also with three presidents—Democrats and Republicans—President Nixon, President Ford, and me.

I think the reason Ed was so successful in bringing this coalition together and in healing the disparities between the White House and Capitol Hill was that when he spoke, you knew at least three things.

First, he deeply believed what he said. Second, he knew what he was talking about. And third, it was the absolute truth.

So I admired him from a distance until the spring of 1972, when Ed was campaigning for president and he came down to Atlanta for a fund-raiser. I invited him to spend the night with me at the governor's mansion—first, because of my admiration for him, and second, because I thought he was going to get the nomination, and he might be looking for a southern governor to be his running mate!

I wanted to make a good impression on him, and I wanted him to think that I was a little more sophisticated than I was.

So late that night, when he was very tired and had been campaigning all day, I said, "Senator, would you like to have a drink?" He said, "Yes, Governor, I believe I would." I said, "Well, what would you like?" And he said, "I'd like scotch and milk."

I was taken aback. I knew about bourbon and branch water and a few other drinks of that kind. But I tried to put on the appearance of being knowledgeable, and I went down to the kitchen to prepare a drink. I got about halfway down the hall when a question came to me. So I went back into the room and, I think, ruined all my chances of being on the ticket. I said, "Is that sweet milk or buttermilk?"

He very gently said, "Sweet milk."

Later, when I was elected president, I looked upon Ed Muskie as one of my closest and most valued advisers. He was still a hero to me, and I turned to him often.

In 1980, as some of you remember, my administration was in trouble. Fifty-three hostages were still being held by militants in Iran. In April we tried to rescue them. My secretary of state, in protest, resigned with a great deal of public fanfare.

I was facing a revolution in my own party from Senator Kennedy and others who were more liberal than I, and it seemed very doubtful that I would even be renominated as an incumbent president. I turned to Ed Muskie, who had a secure seat in the U.S. Senate, and asked him if he would serve as secretary of state.

He said yes. In a way I thought I was doing him a favor. But when I introduced him at the White House as the new secretary of state, he said, "Mr. President, I'm not going to say thanks. I'm going to wait a few months and then decide whether I thank you or not."

He brought to the State Department his formidable knowledge, as a longtime chairman of the Budget Committee, of every domestic and foreign policy program that our nation had. He brought with him, too, that statesmanship from Maine that let the members of our Congress, the people of our nation, and leaders throughout the world know that here was a man who spoke with absolute integrity.

When Prime Minister Ohira of Japan, one of my closest friends, passed away, Ed and I attended his funeral. And on the way back, we stopped in Alaska for a day of fishing, which Ed had suggested as a way for me to forget my troubles. We went to a little lake about an hour and a half from Anchorage and were fishing for grayling. I caught fifteen or twenty. Ed only caught one. After we got through, Ed came up and said, "Mr. President, I'd like to make a comment about the trip." And I waited for him to voice his envy of my good luck. And he said, "You really need to practice your cast." Later he sent me a wonderful fishing rod that I still have.

In the last few days of our administration, it was Ed Muskie's integrity, his sound judgment, his wisdom, his determination, and his patience that made it possible for us to bring every hostage home safe and free. Typically, Ed did not seek any credit for that achievement. He let others take the credit.

I looked up last night the citation that I read when I gave Ed Muskie the Presidential Medal of Freedom: "As senator and secretary of state, candidate, and citizen, Edmund Muskie has captured for himself a place in the public eye and in the public's heart. Devoted to his nation and our ideals, he has performed heroically and with great fortitude in a time of great challenges."

His response was, "You forget that I was also governor."

When asked earlier this week about my friendship with Ed

Muskie, I said that of all the people I've ever known, no one was better qualified to be president of the United States. But, Jane, I'd like to say now that I don't believe many presidents in history have ever contributed as much to the quality of life of people in our nation and around the world as has your husband, Edmund Muskie. I'm grateful to him, and I will miss him immensely.

David Niven

March 1, 1910 ~ July 29, 1983

Tribute by William F. Buckley, written shortly after attending the funeral in Switzerland, *National Review,* August 19, 1983

David Niven

Actor David Niven, christened James David Graham Niven, was born in Kirriemuir, Scotland. A graduate of the Royal Military College at Sandhurst, he served with the British Army in Malta before he resigned his commission and came to Hollywood. He married Primula Rollo in 1940, and the couple had two children before her death in 1946. He married Hjördis Tersmeden in 1948, and they had two daughters.

Signed by Samuel Goldwyn, Niven developed into a polished light-comedian and gallant hero in such films as *The Dawn Patrol* (1938), *Wuthering Heights* (1939), and *Bachelor Mother* (1939). After service as a British Army officer in World War II, he spent thirty years as an urbane leading man, perfectly cast as the gentlemanly voyager Phineas Fogg in *Around the World in 80 Days* (1956), and winning an Academy Award for his portrayal of a deceptive British major in *Separate Tables* (1958). An inimitable raconteur, he wrote his lighthearted memoirs *The Moon's a Balloon* (1972), as well as the nonfiction work about Hollywood, *Bring on the Empty Horses* (1975). In 1981 he wrote the best-selling novel *Go Slowly, Come Back Quickly.*

David Niven died at his home in Switzerland, having suffered from Lou Gehrig's disease for several years.

William F. Buckley

Magazine editor and writer William Frank Buckley Jr. was born in New York City on November 24, 1925, the son of William Frank and Aloise (Steiner) Buckley. He married Patricia Taylor in 1950, and the couple have one child. He earned a B.A. at Yale in 1950.

In 1952, Buckley became associate editor of the *American Mercury,* and in 1955 he founded the *National Review,* serving as its president and editor-in-chief until 1990 and an editor-at-large since 1991. Buckley began a syndicated column in 1962, and since 1966 has been the host of the weekly TV show *Firing Line*. In 1965, Buckley was the Conservative party candidate for mayor of New York City, and was the U.S. delegate to the Twenty-eighth General Assembly of the UN in 1973.

A prolific author, Buckley's works include *Up from Liberalism* (1959), *Right Reason* (1985), *In Search of Anti-Semitism* (1992), and *A Very Private Plot* (1994).

Buckley has been the recipient of many professional awards, including the Presidential Medal of Freedom in 1991 and the Gold Medal award of the National Institute of Social Sciences in 1992.

Mr. Buckley was a longtime friend of Mr. Niven.

Obituary for David Niven by William F. Buckley

CHATEAU D'OEX, SWITZERLAND—St. Peter's (Anglican) Church is small, so that most of the mourners were outside. In other circumstances one would have said that outside there were the gawkers and voyeurs, except that when David Niven died, everyone mourned him, not least villagers among whom he had lived for thirty winters, who knew him also on the screen. The flowers were Hollywood-grand, but different in arrangement from what the Godfather would have ordered for a prominent member of the family. The red-bearded English minister intoned, "Mindful of the example shown to us by our dear departed brother David Niven, let us repeat together the prayer of a sixteenth-century priest, Johann Arndt." It was an absolutely safe bet that David Niven had never heard of Johann Arndt, and there were certainly more movies made by David Niven than sermons listened to by David Niven. Yet it was on the (closed) doors of St. Peter's that he threw himself that November midnight when his daughter was comatose after the terrible car accident.

"Bestow on me, oh Lord, a genial spirit," the priest was reading. On the widow's right sat Prince Rainier, whose own acquaintance with grief was witnessed by the tens of millions without who were present at his wife's funeral. A genial spirit.

There were four at dinner that night, at a restaurant in Monaco, and Rainier was, well, in a grumpy mood. Whatever it is that princes are trained to do to overcome royal distemper was not being done proficiently early on that evening, and this David Niven diagnosed with the speed of an X-ray machine, and, like the physician, David Niven knew his duty, and he did it.

It required about twenty minutes for the therapy totally to take hold. It began with a tale of David's initial encounter with a lady of pleasure, when he was fifteen. It traveled through disparate episodes in Hollywood, Bangkok, Camp David; involving Errol Flynn, Tyrone Power, his cook, his ski teacher. His own naturally high spirits were engaged, but he was ministering primarily to the needy, and the neediest of all in this world are those who suffer not from hunger but from melancholy. He had only the one fear throughout his working life, which was that he might bore somebody, someday. Or that he might fail to stimulate whomever he was talking to. And he had the physician's eye for who, in the room full of people, most needed attention. If ever there was a man who winked at the homely girl, it was Niven.

His friends persuaded him to go to the Mayo Clinic in February 1982. He had been misdiagnosed by half the doctors in Europe, among whom the consensus was that the three or four apparently unrelated things that were happening to him—faintly garbled speech, slight lack of leg coordination, vastly diminished appetite—were owing to a strained nerve dating back to a war injury. In two days, the clinic discovered what it was, and told him—much as Colonel C. Aubrey Smith of the Grenadiers would have told Lieutenant Niven that the expedition against the Russians was probably suicidal—that there was no cure, and that he was entering the "galloping" phase of the disease. Two days later, back in Switzerland, he told his friends that he simply intended to defeat the ridiculous disease, and every day he went for physical therapy.

As his voice control deteriorated, he suffered; but his distinctive exasperation was his relative inability to do his job, which was to be the genial spirit to friends and family.

By the time the next winter came, the last winter, it required concentration to make out what he was saying, but it was still possible, when he spoke slowly. He had, from necessity, become reclusive, but he would go in the afternoons to paint a little on canvases, the last one of which had clouds that, early in February, were pink and white, but, by late March, had become black, and grey, tumultuous even. He was in the hospital before that canvas was completed.

He stepped back one afternoon from his painting. "Do you know, I received a nice letter from a former master at Stowe when he heard I was sick, and I wrote back and said, 'Well, I guess it's just time to pack it in,' and he wrote back"—by now Niven was beginning to laugh—"'What do you mean, "ready to pack it in"? You're only seventy-two. I'm eighty-three and have no intention of packing it in.'" David thought that funny, but then he thought almost everything funny, only now he had to guard against abandoned laughter, because it convulsed him. The last time, again while painting, he could not control himself. "Ran into someone I hadn't seen for years, in Gstaad, and he shouted out from his car, 'Niven, how the hell are you?' And I shouted back as best I could: 'Well, Sam, you see, I got this blood disease-ease—' and he interrupted and said, 'Oh, well, I've got a new bloody car myself!'" Paintbrushes in hand, he doubled over laughing.

Yehudi Menuhin led students in an octet of Mendelssohn's, the congregation recited the Lord's Prayer, and the minister closed by giving thanks that "as an actor and as a writer" the deceased "was able to bring happiness to millions of people the world over. Amen." Amen.

Richard M. Nixon

January 9, 1913 ~ April 22, 1994

Eulogy delivered by President Bill Clinton
at the Richard Nixon Library and Birthplace,
Yorba Linda, California, April 27, 1994

Richard M. Nixon

The thirty-seventh president of the United States, Richard Milhous Nixon was born in Yorba Linda, California, to Quaker parents. Raised in Whittier, he graduated from Whittier College (1934) and received his law degree from Duke University in 1937. He and Patricia Ryan were married in 1940, and had two children, Julie and Tricia.

After several years with a Whittier law firm, Nixon joined the Navy in 1942 and was assigned to duty in the Pacific. Following the war, he won a seat in the House of Representatives in 1946, and was unopposed for reelection in 1948. As a member of the House Un-American Activities Committee, he played a key role in investigating espionage charges against Alger Hiss. After a contentious campaign, Nixon defeated Helen Gahagan Douglas in the U.S. Senate race of 1950. In 1952, Dwight D. Eisenhower selected him as his vice presidential running mate. He was a highly visible spokesman of the administration during his eight-year term. After losing to John F. Kennedy by a razor-thin margin in the 1960 presidential race, Nixon made an unsuccessful bid for governor of California in 1962. He spent the next six years in New York City, where he practiced law and wrote. Among the books written during this period was *Six Crises* (1962).

Vowing to end the war in Vietnam, Nixon returned to the political arena and was elected president in 1968, and won reelection in 1972 by a historic margin. While in office he opened the door to the People's Republic of China, established the Strategic Arms Limitation Talks (SALT) with the Soviet Union, and ended American involvement in Vietnam. At home, Nixon pursued such domestic initiatives as the establishment of the Environmental Protection Agency, the "war on cancer," and the peaceful desegregation of public schools in the South.

In 1973, revelations about the bugging of the Democratic party headquarters during the 1972 campaign implicated administration officials in criminal actions. The Watergate affair grew into a national crisis that, by the summer of 1974, had forced Nixon to release a tape that showed him to be involved in a cover-up plan. In a whirl of public outcry, he resigned from the presidency on August 9, 1974—the first president ever to do so.

After he left the presidency, the Nixons returned to their home in San Clemente, California. The Center for Peace and Freedom, a policy center at the Richard Nixon Library and Birthplace, is dedicated to the perpetuation of his legacy of enlightened national interest in foreign policy and pragmatic idealism at home.

Bill Clinton

The forty-second president of the United States, William Jefferson Clinton was born in Hope, Arkansas, on August 19, 1946. He married Hillary Rodham in 1975, and the couple have one child, Chelsea. Clinton earned a B.A. in international affairs from Georgetown University in 1968, and was a Rhodes scholar at Oxford from 1968 to 1970. He was awarded a J.D. from the Yale Law School in 1973.

Clinton was professor of law at the University of Arkansas from 1973 to 1976, and was elected attorney general for the state of Arkansas in 1976. He became the nation's youngest governor in 1978 and, except for 1980 to 1982, served as the governor of Arkansas until 1992. Bill Clinton became president of the United States in 1993 after defeating President George Bush.

Clinton has been a member of the Task Force on Adolescent Education of the Carnegie Foundation, and from 1990 to 1991 was the chairman of the Democratic Leadership Council.

Bill Clinton was president at the time of Richard Nixon's death.

Eulogy for Richard M. Nixon by Bill Clinton

President Nixon opened his memoirs with a simple sentence: "I was born in a house my father built." Today, we can look back at this little house and still imagine a young boy sitting by the window of the attic he shared with his three brothers, looking out to a world he could then himself only imagine. From those humble roots, as from so many humble beginnings in this country, grew the force of a driving dream—a dream that led to the remarkable journey that ends here today where it all began. Beside the same tiny home, mail-ordered from back East, near this towering oak tree which, back then, was a mere seedling.

President Nixon's journey across the American landscape mirrored that of this entire nation in this remarkable century. His life was bound up with the striving of our whole people, with our crises and our triumphs.

When he became president, he took on challenges here at home on matters from cancer research to environmental protection, putting the power of the federal government where Republicans and Democrats had neglected to put it in the past; in foreign policy. He came to the presidency at a time in our history when Americans were tempted to say we had had enough of the world. Instead, he knew we had to reach out to old friends and old enemies alike. He would not allow America to quit the world.

Remarkably, he wrote nine of his ten books after he left the presidency, working his way back into the arena he so loved by writing and thinking, and engaging us in his dialogue.

For the past year, even in the final weeks of his life, he gave me his wise counsel, especially with regard to Russia. One thing in particular left a profound impression on me. Though this man was in his ninth decade, he had an incredibly sharp and vigorous and rigorous mind.

As a public man, he always seemed to believe the greatest sin was remaining passive in the face of challenges. And he never stopped living by that creed. He gave of himself with intelligence and energy and devotion to duty. And his entire country owes him a debt of gratitude for that service. Oh, yes, he knew great controversy amid defeat as well as victory. He made mistakes; and, they, like his accomplishments, are part of his life and record.

But the enduring lesson of Richard Nixon is that he never gave up being part of the action and passion of his times. He said many times that unless a person has a goal, a new mountain to climb, his spirit will die. Well, based on our last phone conversation and the letter he wrote me just a month ago, I can say that his spirit was very much alive to the very end. That is a great tribute to him, to his wonderful wife, Pat, to his children and to his grandchildren whose love he so depended on and whose love he returned in full measure.

As it is written in the words of a hymn I heard in my church last Sunday: "Grant that I may realize that the trifling of life creates differences, but that in the higher things, we are all one."

In the twilight of his life, President Nixon knew that lesson well. It is, I feel certain, a faith he would want us all to keep. And, so, on behalf of all four former presidents who are here—President Ford, President Carter, President Reagan, President Bush—and on behalf of a grateful nation, we bid farewell to Richard Milhous Nixon.

Helen O'Connell

May 23, 1920 ~ September 9, 1993

Eulogy delivered by Turnley Walker,
St. Paul the Apostle Catholic Church,
Westwood, California, September 11, 1993

Helen O'Connell

Singer Helen O'Connell was born in Lima, Ohio. She was married three times and had four daughters. Her first marriage, in 1941, was to investor Clifford Smith Jr. In 1957 she married author Tom T. Chamales, and her third marriage, in 1991, was to bandleader Frank DeVol.

O'Connell left high school to tour as a big band singer. She joined the Jimmy Dorsey band in 1939, and became one of the most popular singers of the swing era, touring the country throughout the 1940s. Her recording of "Green Eyes" with Bob Eberly sold in the millions.

In the 1950s, O'Connell was the cohost of NBC's *Today Show,* and was hostess of the Miss Universe Pageant for many years. She was also the television spokeswoman for Polaroid cameras. In the late 1970s, she toured the United States with Rose Marie, Margaret Whiting, and Rosemary Clooney in the concert production *4 Girls 4*.

Turnley Walker

A lifelong friend of Helen O'Connell, Turnley Walker has been active in all aspects of the entertainment industry. Primarily a writer of fiction and nonfiction books, Walker also has had considerable quality film and television experience. He is a winner of the Peabody Award, the Sylvania Award, and the Golden Eagle Award for special television programming and educational films.

Walker currently resides with his family in Sherman Oaks, California.

Eulogy for Helen O'Connell by Turnley Walker

One thing you learn as you grow older, then old, is that what is most vibrant and true and pleasing in the young years—the wonder years—can stay with you. The glow, the lilt, the freshness can continue in ways that can be deeply reassuring, and also heartbreaking, since all of life is a balancing between love and less than love.

The most fortunate among us are those who truly keep in their company one person who stays young and loving in a constantly renewing way. And, for us, that person was Helen O'Connell.

Back when the world was young, solely because we were young in it, Helen was the first to find a career spotlight. Or, rather, to have a spotlight find her. And we were delighted! And proud! How she sang on Broadway, on that Strand Theatre stage, with Jimmy Dorsey and Bob Eberle! The golden glow and lilt of it!

That was also the time she began having babies—experiences also shared. There was the evening I went by the hospital to see how Helen was doing with the presentation of her firstborn—and found that, through some mixup, she was waiting it out alone. So, I stayed with her. And stayed.

You made us take our time, Jackie [Helen's daughter]. But you rewarded me greatly. Because in that time together, something extra, in the way of loving friendship, was forged between your mother and me.

The thing is that, through the years, and the decades, Helen stayed young and glowing for all of us. She kept us romantic in the warmest way, couples of us, men and women together. It was like that wonderful old song says: "Each day is Valentine's Day."

When Helen first brought you, Frank [Frank DeVol], to our house, it was as if you had always been there. And the two of you were young together.

Of course, I always thought Helen was singing to me. What man didn't? What unknowable legions of men felt that way? However, nothing diluted what I felt. And loving friendship gave me clear advantages.

For example: The Beverly Hills party casually turmoiling with face-fame people being watchfully polite with one another. The designated entertainer-guest was the female star of a current smash Broadway musical. She sang her hit song to polite applause. I wanted to hear Helen. I mentioned this to the accompanist, suggesting "My Funny Valentine." His eagerness to play for her overrode her reluctance, with several guests joining in. Helen sang and owned the room!

Through the years Helen would come to our house, and I would say, without concern for what might be her mood, "Sing for me."

"Same one?" she'd ask.

"Same one," I'd say.

And she would sing "My Funny Valentine."

You know the words of this lovely, simple, wondrous song:

"My funny Valentine,
Sweet, comic Valentine
You make me smile with my heart."

And there are the song's last words, that I will always hear, in my heart, my smiling heart—always hear Helen singing, forever young and vibrant and loving:

"Each day is Valentine's Day."

Linus Pauling

February 28, 1901 ~ August 19, 1994

Eulogy delivered by Frank Catchpool at a memorial service, Stanford Memorial Church, Stanford, California, August 19, 1994

Linus Pauling

The Nobel Prize–winning chemist and educator Linus Carl Pauling was born in Portland, Oregon, the son of Herman Henry William and Lucy Isabelle (Darling) Pauling. He married Ava Helen Miller in 1923, and they had four children. Pauling was awarded a B.S. from Oregon Agricultural College in Corvallis in 1922, and got his Ph.D. from the California Institute of Technology in 1925.

Pauling taught at the California Institute of Technology from 1927 to 1964, and during his tenure proved himself as one of the most brilliant chemists of the twentieth century. In 1939 he published the landmark work *The Nature of the Chemical Bond,* in which he applied quantum mechanics to chemistry. In 1954, he was awarded the Nobel Prize in chemistry for his contributions to the understanding of chemical bonding. During the fifties and sixties he was an advocate for peace and was instrumental in the banning of nuclear weapons testing. In 1962 he was awarded the Nobel Peace Prize in recognition of these efforts.

After leaving Caltech in 1963, Pauling was a research professor at the Center for the Study of Democratic Institutions, and in 1967 moved to the University of California at San Diego. In 1969 he went to Stanford University. After retiring from Stanford, he founded the Linus Pauling Institute of Science and Medicine in 1973. There, he turned his attention to medicine and investigated the use of megavitamins in the prevention and treatment of disease. In 1970, he published *Vitamin C and the Common Cold,* which triggered a scientific debate over the efficacy of the vitamin in preventing everything from the common cold to cancer.

Frank Catchpool

Physician John Francis Catchpool was born in London, England, on July 16, 1925, to a pacifist Quaker family. He completed his education in England, including medical schools, internship, and residency.

Catchpool served as chief of medical services from 1957 to 1959 with Dr. Albert Schweitzer in Lamberene, Gabon, Africa, where he first met Nobel Laureate Linus Pauling.

Catchpool worked with Pauling at the California Institute of Technology in the department of chemistry. He also held positions at the University of California–San Francisco in its department of pharmacology and as a research epidemiologist.

Returning to Africa, Catchpool was involved in the work of the Schweitzer Foundation and Aid to Biafran Children. He was also project director for the Schweitzer Foundation in Oaxaca, Mexico, aiding Indian children.

Catchpool is the winner of various awards, and has published numerous articles on a variety of subject matter. He is a member of medical academies in England and the United States.

In 1973, Catchpool returned to California and interned at the University of California–San Francisco. In 1974, he became the medical director of the Linus Pauling Institute at Stanford, and since 1975 has operated a "one-stop medical care" clinic as the only practicing primary care physician in Sausalito, California.

Dr. Catchpool was a lifelong friend and colleague of Dr. Pauling.

Eulogy for Linus Pauling by Frank Catchpool

I will speak of Linus as I remember him. At the time I was post doc at Caltech in the early 1960s.

I remember Linus saying that the Nobel Prize for chemistry had been the result of doing things that he enjoyed; fun experimental and theoretical work. But the Nobel Prize for peace resulted from being driven by his convictions that he must, as an informed scientist, speak out against continued and increasing atmospheric nuclear bomb testing.

After the dropping of the Hiroshima bomb, knowledgeable scientists like L.P. were in demand by groups such as Rotary Clubs to explain what "nuclear bomb" meant.

Linus had been in touch with Einstein (who once said: "Linus . . . now there's a genius"). Linus would explain how a critical mass of the uranium isotope could start the chain reaction. He mentioned the number of grams necessary to do this. Later that evening an F.B.I. man arrived at his Altadena home. "You have just given away the most secret secret of the U.S.A. Where did you get that number?" Linus replied, "Well, I just calculated it in my head."

In 1946 Linus wrote his famous book *No More War,* which I have recently reread. The book seems to be full of platitude statements that we can all agree with now. Most of us are now catching up with L.P.

Linus's great contributions to science, medicine, and world peace have come to us in an almost unending stream since his graduate student days at Caltech in 1920.

By the age of thirty he had already published fifty papers on original chemical research. He had become "the chemist's chemist." Predictions of a Nobel Prize were being made by his professor Arthur Noyes in 1931.

Nowadays, so many young people know of Linus only for his steadfast advocacy of megavitamin therapy and know little of his other great contributions to science and medicine.

A chronology of Linus's life and work and the flow of his publications from the structure of amino acids to protein structure are summarized in last week's *New York Times* obituary. I have asked for and received permission to make copies for any of you who did not read it.

Some of my friends think that Linus's work began and ended with megavitamins. The mood of the nation in the 1950s and 1960s was to promote the notion of survivability by preemptive strikes and backyard fallout shelters. School children in the 1950s were taught to "duck and tuck" under their school desks.

M.A.D. (mutual assured destruction) was the policy of the superpowers at that time. We had already been warned by President Eisenhower of the military-industrial complex's power to dictate U.S. policy.

Scientists who should have known better were, I regret to say, reticent. Some of them were profiting from the arms race by working on bomb-science projects.

They were not speaking out. The generals in the Pentagon and the editorial writers were having a clear and unobstructed shot at public thought. We were not getting the input we needed from the scientists who knew about these things.

I was born into a Quaker pacifist family and was working in equatorial Africa as chief resident at the Albert Schweitzer Hospital when one day in 1959 Schweitzer announced that a noted American chemist would be arriving by canoe about noon. "Please come with me to greet him at the river's edge." Albert Schweitzer seemed surprised that I knew of

Linus Pauling. He asked me how I knew of him. I said that I had never met him but that I had read *Time* and *Newsweek,* our only source of information in Africa. In 1959 I was to meet my hero; the scientist with impeccable credentials who could speak with eloquence, authority, lucidity, and simplicity. He was going to spend a week with us in Lamberene. It was to be the high point of my three-and-a-half years in the jungle. At the river's edge I watched the approaching canoe paddled by six lepers. I was expecting to meet an effete European savant or an Ivy League type from an American university. I found him to be a robust outdoorsy quintessentially west American from the backwoods of pioneer Oregonian stock. He fitted right into our primitive rain forest community.

He talked every day for two hours with Schweitzer and then spent some hours touring the hospital with Ava Helen. As they strolled through the hospital hand in hand, they surprised everyone. We were unused to seeing married couples in their late fifties still holding hands.

Linus frequently recalled his first meeting with Ava Helen, his wife of fifty years. He loved to tell how when he was nineteen years old and teaching a class at Oregon State Agricultural College he looked over the list of students in his class and said, "Um . . . Miss Miller, would you please tell me about ammonium hydroxide." A bright attractive young lady jumped up and answered his question perfectly. Linus noted her name and started writing notes to her on her term papers. Nowadays this would be called sexual harassment. He loved to tease her that his finger on the student list might have lit on Betty Boop instead of Ava Helen Miller. They married when Linus got his Ph.D. at age twenty-one. She was his loyal associate and instigator of some of his enterprises. I will talk later of how she influenced some of his thinking.

As we toured the hospital and Pauling watched me work with the Africans, he talked about sickle cell anemia. I had thirty or so patients with huge purulent ulcers on their legs. I know now that these mostly accompany sickle cell anemia. Linus talked with my colleagues, telling us the story of the genetic aberration that Itano and he had discovered that caused the misplacement of a single amino acid in the 130 amino acid sequence of the hemoglobin molecule. He said that you could call this a disease of the molecules. A molecular disease . . . a strange idea, I thought. I had never heard the term before.

With tutelage from Pauling, Schweitzer became knowledgeable in nuclear physics and fallout from nuclear bomb testing and its contribution to genetic damage and disease.

Later Schweitzer's famous appeal to the United Nations was broadcast from Oslo, but blocked out in the United States.

Schweitzer had said to me, "I remember the eruption of Krakatoa in 1883." He remembered the clouds of dust thrown in the stratosphere which were to rain down on Europe months later. I thought . . . yeah, that's what fallout is like. It astounded me that Schweitzer, aged eighty-nine, could remember headlines that he had read in 1883.

One day Pauling said to me, "Come to Caltech on your next leave. There are many things happening in biology and genetics which doctors now being trained will not understand. They are going to be left behind in years to come."

On leave from Africa I arrived at Caltech in January 1960. It was indeed an exciting place where one could sit down to lunch at the greasy spoon with one or two Nobelists and three or four future Nobelists. There were lectures given by Robert Oppenheimer, Roger Sperry and Dick Fyneman, Murray Gelman, Watson and Crick, and other famous scientists.

The DNA code was just unrolling before my very eyes. The molecular biology of molecular diseases and molecular solutions to molecular diseases were being mooted. There was even talk of a possible department of molecular pharmacology at UCSF. However, I believe the idea was nixed as an absurdity for a medical center devoted to surgery, medical therapy, and infectious disease, to have a department of molecular anything.

In 1961 I felt a surprising reluctance of his colleagues to associate with Linus's statements about the dangers of nuclear fallout and his call for an end to atmospheric testing of nuclear bombs. I heard it said several times that scientists should stick to science and stay out of politics.

There were even McCarthy-like mutterings that Pauling was aiding and abetting the Russians.

Although privately agreeing with Pauling, many close friends and colleagues were embarrassed and sometimes offended by his public statements.

Friends of the Paulings that I met in Pasadena would say, "Oh yes. You work for Linus. We used to swim in their swimming pool but we don't see them often now. He is so outspoken." These words hurt me as they must have hurt Linus and Ava Helen.

The prevailing atmosphere was that physicists and chemists should stick to their sciences. Scientists should not offer gratuitous advice to the almighty military and our wise state department and should believe whatever our all-knowing CIA chose to tell us.

Once or twice I wondered whether there were pieces of information that I was not aware of. Maybe there were secret developments in nuclear physics that I was ignorant of which would allow Edward Teller and other scientists to claim that a little radiation was good for you.

Shortly after arriving in Pasadena, I remember going to the

Each wall of the office carried an X-ray machine. The dentist took many X-rays of my teeth. He said to me, "There is a guy named Pauling down at Caltech who is going to make us wear lead aprons, and shield the technicians behind leaded walls. That man says that radiation is not good for you."

All this has come to pass and it was Linus's words that started it all.

But how could his peers and colleagues who worked closely with him let him stand alone? Some of them, of course, had obvious conflicts of interest since they were working on bomb science and were supported by grants from the D.O.D.

Radio and TV debates with Teller and his ilk usually ended in bluster, innuendos, and obfuscations as debaters wrapped themselves in the flag or with privileged secret knowledge.

In 1961 came the absurd "Congressional testing of Linus Pauling" by the Senate Internal Security Subcommittee chaired by Senator Dodds. This was a preposterous attack on all scientists and all intellects.

For instance, on day one of the subcommittee, Pauling was questioned at just the right moment so that the questions but not the answers could meet the press deadlines. He was asked, "Will you give us the list of all people who have signed your petition?" Linus replied, "You already have the list and it is on public view at the United Nations."

The next day . . . "Will you give us a list of all those to whom you sent petitions?" There was a deathly silence as many wondered . . . "Is he going to answer this one or not?" Linus replied, "Of course I will give you a list. Nobody is responsible for the mail he receives."

The third day the questions became more specific. "Will you give us the names of those who collected the most signatures?" Everyone waited to see if Linus was going to jail for the guts to refuse to answer, and probably go to jail for contempt of Congress. "No," he said. "I am not going to answer that question because many of those signatures were collected by young high-minded graduate students or professors at the threshold of their careers. The committee has the power to control and blight their futures in science. And I am not going to answer that."

He was told that if he did not answer he would be in contempt of Congress and could be jailed as other protesters had been jailed.

I met Linus as he returned from Washington. He told me somewhat ruefully that he would consider going to jail if Ava Helen could go with him. "Maybe I could take the children to jail so we could remain a happy family," he said.

Rumors at that time in the Caltech greasy spoon were that a rich trustee had offered a two million dollar gift with one string attached; "that Communist Professor Pauling must be fired." The provost is said to have explored that possibility but found that a tenured professor cannot be fired. It seems to me that the Caltech community should have rushed to his defense.

I was constantly amazed that a man could continue to function under such stress. All this time scientific papers were pouring out of his office. Freshman chemistry classes were given, speeches and statements made, textbooks written and revised. Others have noted how Pauling, with his feet on the desk, could dictate chapters of his textbook, complete with references, formulae, and equations. When asked how much revision he would have to do before printing, he replied, "None . . . except to correct my secretary's mistakes."

When I asked a question, Linus would often lean back in his chair to pull out a drawer of one of his ten file cabinets. Pulling out a paper, he would say, "Let's see . . . I wrote about that in 1939." And it seemed that every other day he had to dash off to Washington to appear before a hostile Senate committee.

The issues Pauling raised about fallout, genetic damage, endocrine disease, mental retardation, the stupidity of backyard bomb shelters and of training children to believe nuclear war would come and go . . . And that we would be victorious and live happily ever after . . . are no longer contested.

There are now no secrets in bomb manufacture. Everyone seems to know how to make a bomb. Once in 1962 I asked a young nuclear physicist friend at Caltech to tell me what it would cost me if I were an Arab sheik with unlimited millions, to hire a scientist and equipment to make an atom bomb. He said, "I'll think about that." He came back two days later and said, "Probably a billion would do it." It was only a matter of time before the nuclear club would be extended to include terrorist nations and that an agreement to end atmospheric bomb testing was obviously the first step. His logic was so simple and the fact so obvious that they could not be denied. Why were not more of his colleagues speaking out with him?

Once I asked a grad student, "Are you going to hear Linus talk at the student union this evening?" And he replied, "I think I'll wash my car." I told him that he was missing the experience of a lifetime.

Once in the chemistry office I was told that the research grant bookkeeping was not up to date. "I love Linus," the secretary said, "But I wish he would drop the politics and get back to chemistry." Of course, the error was later to be found in the chemistry office, not Linus's error.

One day in 1963 as I drove my car to the Gates and Crellin Chemistry Lab at Caltech, I heard a news flash from Oslo on my car radio saying that the Nobel Peace Prize for 1962 had been awarded to Linus Pauling. At last, I rejoiced, confirmation that indeed the world was listening, and credit for the promotion of the atmospheric bomb test ban treaty between JFK and Kruschev was in part due to Linus's tireless and selfless campaign.

For his endless reiteration of the obvious scientific facts and his call for an end of atmospheric testing by the great powers he had endured the loss of academic support . . . even faced imprisonment.

It was a happy moment.

As I stood there by my car listening to the radio, I grabbed a startled professor who was passing by and said, "Listen to the radio." And as we listened a crestfallen look came to his face . . . a look not of joy or relief, but a look of anguish. His expression seemed to say, "What have we done to him? Why were we not supporting him while the Nobel Prize committee and millions around the world were listening?"

In 1954 the chemistry prize had brought on a torchlight parade and a bonfire and a student-written review and roast to acclaim their beloved professor. This time, however, a greater honor was met with a glum silence.

One week later Max Delbruck asked me if I knew of any chemistry department plans to honor Linus, and I knew of none. Max said, "Biology would like to do something. What should we do?" I was being asked by a chairman of a division of Caltech of chemistry's intentions and I was only a graduate student. "Well," I said, "Announce your plans as quickly as possible. The hurtful silence to L.P. must be terrible." Later, a large videotaping truck from *Time-Life* magazine was crammed into the courtyard of the Gates and Crellin Lab. The television interview began. I could see the cables from the truck to his office. After a while, Linus came to my little lab. He looked sad, but not angry.

"I asked them," he said, "Why should I continue the interview, if the editorial is going to be derogatory? The reporters are now telephoning their editors."

L.P. left my lab and came back a few minutes later. "They tell me they are sorry but the editorial has already been written and they say that it is derogatory."

Three days later, a *Life* editorial headed "A Weird Insult from Norway" appeared on the newsstands. Later biology gave a well-attended tea party and wine tasting in the biology courtyard. As I looked at the scene I thought, "We have all been Judas. We let him stand alone." That was the unspoken prevailing thought that sunny afternoon in the biology courtyard.

Now, as I read my *New York Times* and listen to the PBS radio station, every time I hear the news . . . one thousand mirved ICBMs with nuclear bombs have been pointed away from the United States. . . . Now plutonium can be bought on the black market. . . . Who owns the missiles in Siberia? . . . What are North Korea's and Pakistan's intentions? . . . Does Israel have the bomb? . . . Do all Mideast countries have the bomb? The Bikini Atoll is still so hot that the Marshall Islanders cannot be allowed to go home. . . . Frightening stories of nuclear accidents around the world . . . of death and congenital malformations at Semiplatinsk . . . of troops deliberately exposed to radiation in the 1950s . . . unexplained rising death rates from leukemia. . . . Each day I hear the news I think, "L.P. said it thirty years ago. Now we all agree with him. There is no argument left. Where is the subcommittee who persecuted him and threatened him with jail?"

I say . . . he was a prophet . . . with honor in his time.

Norman Vincent Peale

May 31, 1898 ~ December 24, 1993

Eulogy delivered by Margaret Peale Everett at the funeral,
Marble Collegiate Church, New York City,
December 29, 1993

Norman Vincent Peale

The Reverend Dr. Norman Vincent Peale was born in Bowersville, Ohio, the son of Charles Clifford and Anna (Delancy) Peale. He married Ruth Stafford in 1930, and the couple had three children. Peale was granted an A.B. from Ohio Wesleyan University in 1920, and a D.D. in 1936. He also earned an S.T.B. and an A.M. in 1924 from Boston University.

Peale was ordained as a minister in the Methodist Episcopal Church in 1922, and first served as pastor in Berkeley, Rhode Island. In 1924 he moved to a church in Brooklyn, and served the University Methodist Church in Syracuse, New York, until 1932. In 1932 he was appointed pastor of the Marble Collegiate Reformed Church in New York City, where he remained until his retirement in 1984.

One of the nation's most effective religious figures for over three decades, Dr. Peale reached millions with his sermons, books, and radio and television programs. Exhorting people to feel better about their lives, he was one of the first clergymen to combine psychiatry with religion.

Peale was a prolific author. Among his best-known books are *A Guide to Confident Living* (1948), which was his first best-seller, and *The Power of Positive Thinking* (1952), one of the highest-selling religious titles in publishing history. The last of his forty-one books, *This Incredible Century,* was published in 1991.

Dr. Peale was the recipient of numerous awards, including five Freedom Foundation awards, the Horatio Alger award in 1952, and the 1984 Presidential Medal of Freedom.

Margaret Peale Everett

Margaret Peale Everett is the oldest child of Norman Vincent Peale and his wife Ruth Stafford Peale. She is active in her church, where she is an elder, member of the personnel committee, and coordinator of small groups. She is also involved in many community volunteer activities and serves on the board of directors of *Guideposts* (the magazine and publishing company), Faith at Work (an interdenominational Christian ministry), and the Stony Brook School (a Christian boarding/day school). She works with Peale Center, the ministry arm of *Guideposts,* on a number of special projects, and for many years has been on the staff of its School of Practical Christianity for ministers and their spouses. She has conducted workshops on small groups and has led conferences with her husband, Paul, a Presbyterian minister. Maggie and Paul live in Pittsburgh, Pennsylvania, and have two children and two grandchildren.

Eulogy for Norman Vincent Peale by Margaret Peale Everett

How do you say goodbye to someone you love? One week ago I said goodbye to my father as I left his bedside to return to my home in Pittsburgh. I told him how much I loved him and how blessed I had been to have him as a father. That was a tangible goodbye. Today is another form of goodbye. Funerals are not for the deceased, who have already been released from the limitations of this world. Funerals are for the rest of us—those family and friends and admirers who are left behind. We grieve; we feel loss; we have to adjust to a new reality. We hope this service will help you to say goodbye to a very special man we all loved and admired.

Who was Norman Vincent Peale? Who was my father? He was a man of abundant energy, and, until the last year and a half, abundant good health. He was a simple man whose small town roots and values never left him in spite of living in New York City almost his entire adult life. He was gracious, loving, and available to everyone, be they an employee, a corporation president, or an ordinary person. He was intensely loyal to his friends and family, and he had the biggest heart of anyone I've ever known. People responded to him with gifts from the heart because he touched their lives from his heart. The most recent example was just last week. Richard, Dad's weekday caregiver, said to me, "I don't know what to get your father for Christmas." I told him that his loving care was gift enough. Then on December 23rd, Richard said to my mother that he wanted to come in and work on Christmas Day as his gift to Dad. He wanted to give from his heart to a man he not only worked for but loved as well. Unfortunately, he never got that opportunity.

Dad could be moody and feisty at times and he was a workaholic.

But he was also loving, tender, funny, and entertaining. From my earliest recollection he loved to hug us. I remember big bear hugs where you were enveloped in his arms. In his last months hugs were an important part of our communication, hopefully for him but most definitely for us. He had a lively sense of humor and was a master storyteller. The secret of his sense of humor was part timing, part ability to paint a picture with words, part self-depreciation. Several of his best stories are so good, and have been told so often, that we, his family, can recount them by heart, word-for-word—and we still laugh.

When we were children he entertained us with original stories every night at dinner. Each episode of a trio called Larry, Harry, and Perry and their magic airplane delighted us, and we clamored for more.

Dad had a deep personal faith that was rooted in the belief that Jesus Christ can change lives. He first saw this in action as a young boy when the town drunk went forward at a service in his father's church in Ohio and later became the town's leading citizen. His own spiritual journey was punctuated with a series of profound inner changes, and he never ceased to bring his own frailties to Christ for healing and transformation. As a college student he had a debilitating fear of public speaking. One of his favorite Bible verses was Psalms 34:4, "I sought the Lord and He heard me and delivered me from all my fears." He had personal experience of such deliverance through the power of God. While he never completely shed his inferiority complex, he used it to identify with people. When he told how Christ had changed him, people believed that Christ could change them, too.

Dad believed that each of us can do so much more if we do not limit ourselves by fear. He never gave me much advice, but once I told him I was afraid to take on a certain job because I didn't think I could do it. He told me, "If you never stretch yourself beyond what you think you can do, you'll never know how much you can do." Then he paraphrased Psalms 34:4, "Ask the Lord to help you and He will take your fear away."

Dad really hated growing old, although I think he would have enjoyed hitting the century mark. When someone complimented him on turning ninety, he said it was no big deal. It just meant you weren't dead yet. He hated not being able to make speeches anymore, something he did about as well as anybody who ever lived. We tried to get him to slow down when he was about eighty, but he paid no attention to that well-meaning advice. He knew that he derived energy and purpose from using the gift God had given to him.

Dad faced many challenges in his life. He had his critics and got himself in and out of hot water a number of times. Because of his acute sensitivity he was deeply hurt by several of these experiences. However,

I believe his greatest challenge was in facing his declining physical condition and loss of activity the last year of his life. Those of us closest to him know how difficult this time was for him and what an adjustment it required of him. Therefore, we can only rejoice that his new life has begun and that he has been made whole once again. The evangelist Dwight L. Moody said in an interview in 1899, "Someday you will read in the papers that Dwight L. Moody is dead. Don't you believe a word of it. At that moment I will be more alive than I am now." I believe that is true of Dad today.

At a memorial service on Monday at Peale Center, one of the staff members sang a beautiful song which spoke to me of Dad's life:

> O when I come to the end of my journey
> Weary of life and the battle is won
> Carrying the staff and the cross of redemption
> He'll understand and say, "Well done."

So, how do you say goodbye to someone you love? You don't. You simply say thanks for the memories, thanks for the privilege of sharing your life, and thanks for the profound lessons you taught by the kind of person you were.

Yitzhak Rabin

March 1, 1922 ~ November 4, 1995

Eulogy delivered by King Hussein at the state funeral,
Jerusalem, Israel

Yitzhak Rabin

The prime minister of Israel, Yitzhak Rabin was born in Jerusalem. He married Lea Schlossberg, with whom he had two children. From 1936 to 1940, he was a student at the Kadoorie Agricultural School at Kfar Tabor (Israel), and received an honorary Ph.D. from Hebrew University of Jerusalem in 1967.

At age nineteen, Rabin joined the Palestinian Jewish militia, Haganah, and was assigned to the Hebrew underground command force, Palmach. Until the late sixties, Rabin was a military hero whose talents as a tactician contributed to Israel's rise to power in the Middle East. During this period he was the head of tactical operations headquarters (1950 to 1953), head of the training department of the Israel Defense Force (1954 to 1956), and army chief of staff (1964 to 1968).

In 1968, Rabin made a successful transition from the military field to the political arena. He served as Israeli ambassador to the United States until 1973, and became a member of the Knesset in 1974. Rabin was appointed the minister of labor in 1974, and that same year became the first native-born prime minister of Israel. He resigned in 1977, and between 1981 and 1990 served two more terms as minister of defense. Rabin became prime minister again in 1992, and in 1994 signed a historical accord with PLO leader Yasir Arafat, allowing for Palestinian self-rule in Gaza and the West Bank. Together with Arafat and Israeli defense minister Shimon Peres, Rabin was awarded the Nobel Peace Prize in 1994.

Rabin was assassinated in 1995 at a Tel Aviv peace rally.

King Hussein

His Majesty Hussein Bin Talal I, King of Jordan, was born in Amman, Jordan, on November 14, 1935, the son of Crown Prince Talal and Zein.

Hussein has been married four times and is the father of eleven children. He is currently married to Lisa Halaby (Queen Noor) and together they have four children. Hussein began his formal education in Alexandria, Egypt, at Victoria College, and continued at the Harrow School in England. From 1952 to 1953, King Hussein studied at the Royal Military Academy in Sandhurst, England.

Hussein became king in 1953, after his father was proclaimed mentally unfit to rule. Although he has pursued unity with the other Arab countries, Hussein has also sought a moderate, pro-Western course. He led Jordan through the Arab-Israeli War in 1967, and the civil war with the PLO in 1970, but since then has remained neutral in regional conflicts.

Hussein is the author of *Uneasy Lies the Head* (1962), *My War with Israel* (1969), and *Mon Metierde Roi* (1975). He has been awarded the Order Al-Nahda, the Order Al-Hawkab, the Order Al-Istiqial, and numerous other decorations.

Eulogy for Yitzhak Rabin by King Hussein

I never thought that the moment would come like this, when I would grieve the loss of a brother, a colleague and a friend, a man, a soldier who met us on the opposite side of a divide, who we respected as he respected us. A man I came to know because I realize, as he did, that we had to cross over the divide, establish the dialogue, and strive to leave also . . . a legacy that is worthy of him.

And so we became brethren and friends.

You lived as a soldier. You died as a soldier for peace, and I believe it is time for all of us to come out openly and to speak to the camp of peace. . . . We believe that our one God wishes us to live in peace and wishes peace upon us. For these are his teachings to all of the followers of the three great monotheistic religions.

Let our voices rise high to speak of our commitment to peace for all times to come and let us tell those who live in darkness, who are the enemies of light and true faith and religion and the teachings of our one God.

Maybe God will bless you with the realization that you must join it, and we pray that you will. But otherwise, we are not ashamed, nor are we afraid, nor are we anything but determined to conclude the legacy for which my friend fell, as did my grandfather, in this very city, when I was with him as but a young boy.

He was a man of courage, a man of vision, and he was endowed with one of the greatest virtues that any man can have. He was endowed with humility.

He had courage. He had vision, and he had a commitment to peace.

And, standing here, I commit before you, before my people in Jordan and before the world, myself to continue to do the utmost to ensure that we shall leave a similar legacy.

So many live, and so many inevitably die. . . . But those who are fortunate and lucky in life are those who leave something behind. And you are such a man, my friend.

People who once were your enemies are somber today.

As long as I live, I will be proud to have known him, to have worked with him as a brother, as a friend, and as a man.

Sam Rayburn

January 6, 1882 ~ November 16, 1961

Tribute by Congressman James Roosevelt at a memorial service, U.S. Congress, and appearing as part of the *Congressional Record*

Sam Rayburn

Speaker of the House Sam Rayburn was born in Roane County, Tennessee, the son of William Marion and Martha Waller Rayburn. After earning a B.S. at East Texas College, he studied law at the University of Texas, and began his legal practice in Bonham, Texas.

Rayburn began his long political career in 1906, when he was elected to the Texas House of Representatives as a Democrat. In 1912 he was elected to the U.S. Congress, and served there for forty-eight years—the longest membership in the House. Rayburn became majority leader in 1937, and was elected Speaker of the House in 1940. Except for two periods (1947 to 1949 and 1953 to 1955), he held the position for seventeen years, surpassing all previous speakerships. A parliamentarian, Rayburn was one of the strongest Speakers in U.S. history, serving throughout the administrations of Presidents Franklin Delano Roosevelt, Harry S Truman, and John F. Kennedy.

James Roosevelt

For a biographical sketch of James Roosevelt, see his eulogy, page 155. James Roosevelt served with Speaker Rayburn in Congress.

Tribute for Sam Rayburn by James Roosevelt

Mr. Speaker, today we are assembled to pay honor and respect to the late Speaker of the House of Representatives, Sam Rayburn, of Texas. Our tribute to him is not offered merely in recognition of the high position among us which he attained and held for so long—longer than any previous Speaker. Nor do we gather to honor him merely because of his long and continuous service to his country here in the House—longer than any member here present. But rather we gather to take note of all these things. So recall again the essential greatness that was in the man, Sam Rayburn. He possessed a warmth of personality, a humility of spirit, and a quality of strength that is rare in men of this life. He was, in every sense, a great man; we honor him accordingly.

Sam Rayburn's life was dedicated, as Lincoln defined, "to the proposition that all men are created equal"; not equal, perhaps, in physical power; not equal in intellectual endowments; not equal either in moral fiber; but without regard to differences of race, color, or religion; equal in the right and opportunity to enjoy the blessings of freedom in a nation whose laws and systems undertake to guarantee the equal enjoyment of every right to those who support and defend it. Sam Rayburn's life was dedicated to these principles for future generations as well.

Before I became a member of Congress, while serving in the executive branch, I remember well the contribution of Speaker Sam Rayburn as the author and architect and ever vigilant guardian of such great measures as the Rural Electrification Administration, the Tennessee Valley Authority, and other so-called New Deal measures that perhaps saved America in those days from disintegration and losses which might have been irretrievable.

To Sam Rayburn, too, must go a word of credit for his ability to keep us, the Democratic Party, a united national party. Under his leadership, election after election, Democratic majorities were won in the House even when we lost presidential elections. He was a Democrat, yes, a partisan one who never lost the respect and trust of every member of the opposition party.

Sam Rayburn's love for his country and its ideals was certainly great, but no less great was his love and respect for this body. He served long in the halls of the house of Congress and his love and devotion to this House and to its purpose grew with each day of service. The House has lost in him a great member, and we, as members of this body, have lost a great and good friend.

In our grief, let us take new courage on this day of sadness; with unity and determination let us move forward to the attainment of the goal which he set for us and toward which he led us, not only here but throughout the nation and the world.

As we contemplate anew the humane purpose in the lives of men, let us remember that gentle spirit, now departed, and his purpose, and let us renew our efforts toward that end.

Eleanor Roosevelt

October 12, 1882 ~ November 7, 1962

Eulogy delivered by Adlai E. Stevenson at a memorial service, Cathedral of St. John the Divine, New York City, November 17, 1962

Eleanor Roosevelt

Anna Eleanor Roosevelt was born in New York City, the niece of Theodore Roosevelt and wife of Franklin D. Roosevelt, who she married in 1905. She took up extensive political work during her husband's illness from polio, and proved herself an invaluable social adviser to him when he became president.

In 1941, she became assistant director of the office of civilian defense. After her husband's death in 1945 she extended the scope of her activities, and was a delegate to the United Nations General Assembly (1945 to 1951) and chairperson of the UN Human Rights Commission (1946 to 1951). In 1961, she was reappointed to the General Assembly by President John F. Kennedy.

Eleanor Roosevelt is the author of several books, including *This Is My Story* (1937), *The Moral Basis of Democracy* (1940), *On My Own* (1958), and her *Autobiography* (1962).

Adlai E. Stevenson

For a biographical sketch of Adlai Stevenson, see his eulogy, page 163. Stevenson's eulogy for Eleanor Roosevelt has been acknowledged as one of the most outstanding speeches of our time.

Eulogy for Eleanor Roosevelt by Adlai E. Stevenson

One week ago this afternoon, in the Rose Garden at Hyde Park, Eleanor Roosevelt came home for the last time. Her journeys are over. The remembrance now begins.

In gathering here to honor her, we engage in a self-serving act. It is we who are trying, by this ceremony of tribute, to deny the fact that we have lost her, and, at least, to prolong the farewell, and—possibly—to say some of the things we dared not say in her presence, because she would have turned aside such testimonial with impatience and gently asked us to get on with some of the more serious business of the meeting.

A grief perhaps not equaled since the death of her husband seventeen years ago is the world's best tribute to one of the great figures of our age—a woman whose lucid and luminous faith testified always for sanity in an insane time and for hope in a time of obscure hope—a woman who spoke for the good toward which man aspires in a world which has seen too much of the evil of which man is capable.

She lived seventy-eight years, most of the time in tireless activity, as if she knew that only a frail fragment of the things that cry out to be done could be done in the lifetime of even the most fortunate. One has the melancholy sense that when she knew death was at hand, she was contemplating not what she achieved, but what she had not quite managed to do. And I know she wanted to go—when there was no more strength to do.

Yet how much she had done, how much still unchronicled. We dare not try to tabulate the lives she salvaged, the battles, known and unrecorded, she fought, the afflicted she comforted, the hovels she brightened, the faces and places, near and far, that were given some new radiance, some sound of music, by her endeavors. What other single human being has touched and transformed the existence of so many others? What better measure is there of the impact of anyone's life?

There was no sick soul too wounded to engage her mercy. There was no signal of human distress which she did not view as a personal summons. There was no affront to human dignity from which she fled because the timid cried "Danger." And the number of occasions on which her intervention turned despair into victory we may never know.

Her life was crowded, restless, fearless. Perhaps she pitied most not those whom she aided in the struggle, but the more fortunate who were preoccupied with themselves and cursed with the self-deceptions of private success. She walked in the slums and the ghettos of the world, not on a tour of inspection, nor as a condescending patron, but as one who could not feel complacent while others were hungry, and who could not find contentment while others were in distress. This was not sacrifice; this, for Mrs. Roosevelt, was the only meaningful way of life.

These were not conventional missions of mercy. What rendered this unforgettable woman so extraordinary was not merely her response to suffering; it was her comprehension of the complexity of the human condition.

Not long before she died, she wrote that "within all of us there are two sides. One reaches for the stars, the other descends to the level of beasts." It was, I think, this discernment that made her so unfailingly tolerant of friends who faltered and led her so often to remind the smug and complacent that "there but for the grace of God."

But we dare not regard her as just a benign incarnation of good works. For she was not only a great woman and a great humanitarian, but a great democrat. I use the word with a small "d"—though it was, of course, equally true that she was a great Democrat with a capital "D." When I say she was a great small "d" democrat, I mean that she had a lively and astute understanding of the nature of the democratic process. She was a master political strategist with a fine sense of humor. And, as she said, she loved a good fight.

She was a realist. Her compassion did not become sentimentality. She understood that progress was a long labor of compromise. She mistrusted absolutism in all its forms—the absolutism of the word and even more the absolutism of the deed. She never supposed that all the problems of life could be cured in a day or a year or a lifetime. Her pungent and salty understanding of human behavior kept her always in intimate contact with reality. I think this was a primary source of her strength, because she never thought that the loss of a battle meant the loss of a war, nor did she suppose that a compromise which produced only part of the objective sought was an act of corruption or of treachery. She knew that no formula of words, no combination of deeds, could abolish the troubles of life overnight and usher in the millennium.

The miracle, I have tried to suggest, is how much tangible good she really did; how much realism and reason were mingled with her instinctive compassion; how her contempt for the perquisites of power ultimately won her the esteem of so many of the powerful; and how, at her death, there was a universality of grief that transcended all the harsh boundaries of political, racial, and religious strife and, for a moment at least, united men in a vision of what their world might be.

We do not claim the right to enshrine another mortal, and this least of all would Mrs. Roosevelt have desired. She would have wanted it said, I believe, that she well knew the pressures of pride and vanity, the sting of bitterness and defeat, the gray days of national peril and personal anguish. But she clung to the confident expectation that men could fashion their own tomorrow if they could only learn that yesterday can be neither relived nor revised.

Many who have spoken of her in these last few days have used a word to which we all assent, because it speaks a part of what we feel. They have called her a lady, a great lady, the First Lady of the world. But the word "lady," though it says much about Eleanor Roosevelt, does not say all. To be incapable of self-concern is not a negative virtue; it is the other side of a coin that has a positive face—the most positive, I think, of all the faces. And to enhance the humanity of others is not a kind of humility; it is a kind of pride—the noblest of all the forms of pride. No man or woman can respect other men and women who does not respect life. And to respect life is to love it. Eleanor Roosevelt loved life—and that, perhaps, is the most meaningful thing that can be said about her, for it says so much beside.

It takes courage to love life. Loving it demands imagination and perception and the kind of patience women are more apt to have than men—the bravest and most understanding women. And loving it takes something more beside—it takes a gift for life, a gift for love.

Eleanor Roosevelt's childhood was unhappy—miserably unhappy, she sometimes said. But it was Eleanor Roosevelt who also said that "one must never, for whatever reason, turn his back on life." She did not mean that duty should compel us. She meant that life should. "Life," she said, "was meant to be lived." A simple statement. An obvious statement. But a statement that by its obviousness and its simplicity challenges the most intricate of all the philosophies of despair.

Many of the admonitions she bequeathed us are neither new thoughts nor novel concepts. Her ideas were, in many respects, old fashioned—as old as the Sermon on the Mount, as the reminder that it is more blessed to give than to receive, as the words of St. Francis that she loved so well: "For it is in the giving that we receive."

She imparted to the familiar language—nay, what too many have come to treat as the cliches—of Christianity a new poignancy and vibrance. She did so not by reciting them, but by proving that it is possible to live them. It is this above all that rendered her unique in her century. It was said of her contemptuously at times that she was a do-gooder, a charge leveled with similar derision against another public figure 1,962 years ago.

We who are assembled here are of various religious and political faiths, and perhaps different conceptions of man's destiny in the universe. It is not an irreverence, I trust, to say that the immortality Mrs. Roosevelt would have valued most would be found in the deeds and visions of her life inspired in others, and in the proof that they would be faithful to the spirit of any tribute conducted in her name.

And now one can almost hear Mrs. Roosevelt saying that the speaker has already talked too long. So we must say farewell. We are always saying farewell in this world—always standing at the edge of loss attempting to retrieve some memory, some human meaning, from the silence—something which was precious and is gone.

Often, although we know the absence well enough, we cannot name it or describe it even. What left the world when Lincoln died: Speaker after speaker in those aching days tried to tell his family or his neighbors or his congregation. But no one found the words, not even Whitman. "When lilacs last in the dooryard bloomed" can break the heart, but not with Lincoln's greatness, only with his loss. What the words could never capture was the man himself. His deeds were known; every schoolchild knew them. But it was not his deeds the country mourned; it was the man—the mastery of life which made the greatness of the man.

It was always so. On that April day when Franklin Roosevelt died, it was not a president we wept for. It was a man. In Archibald MacLeish's words:

"Fagged out, worn down, sick. With the weight of his own bones, the task finished, the war won, the victory assured, the glory left behind him for the others. (And the wheels roll up through the night in the sweet land in the cool air in the spring between the lanterns)."

It is so now. What we have lost in Eleanor Roosevelt is not her life. She lived that out to the full. What we have lost, what we wish to recall for ourselves, to remember, is what she was herself. And who can name it? But she left "a name to shine on the entablatures of truth, forever."

We pray that she has found peace, and a glimpse of sunset. But today we weep for ourselves. We are lonelier; someone has gone from one's own life—who was like the certainty of refuge; and someone has gone from the world—who was like a certainty of honor.

James Roosevelt

December 23, 1907 ~ August 13, 1991

Eulogy delivered by the Reverend Kenneth E. McMillan,
Newport Center United Methodist Church,
Newport, California, August 18, 1991

James Roosevelt

Ex-Congressman and business consultant James Roosevelt was born in New York City, the eldest son of Franklin Delano and Anna Eleanor Roosevelt. He was married four times and was the father of seven children. Roosevelt graduated from Harvard in 1930, and while attending Boston University organized Roosevelt & Sargent, Inc., an insurance company based in Boston. He served as its president until 1937, resigning to work for his father's reelection campaign. He accepted a position in the administration, and remained there until the U.S. entered World War II. Roosevelt served in the U.S. Marine Corps from 1940 to 1945, and served at Guadalcanal and the second Battle of Midway. He was decorated with the Navy Cross and the Silver Star.

After the war, Roosevelt became president of James Roosevelt & Co. of Corona Del Mar, California.

Roosevelt is the author of *Affectionately, F.D.R.* (1959), *My Parents* (1976), and *A Family Matter* (1979).

Kenneth E. McMillan

The Reverend Kenneth E. McMillan was born in Santa Barbara, California. He and his wife, Patty, have two children, Jerry and Kathy. He received a bachelor of arts in music from the University of California, Santa Barbara, in 1958, and a bachelor of divinity from the Iliff School of Theology in 1961.

From 1961 to 1963, he was pastor at San Luis Obispo Methodist Church, and from 1963 to 1968 at Garvanza Methodist Church in Los Angeles. Moving to the Fountain Valley United Methodist Church in 1968, he was pastor there until 1971, at which point he became minister at the

Sierra Madre congregation, a post he held until 1978. From 1978 to 1984 he held the pastorate at the Newport Center United Methodist Church of Corona Del Mar.

From 1984 to the present, he has been senior minister of Los Altos United Methodist Church in Long Beach. He is the past president of the Council on Finance and Administration of the California-Pacific Conference of the United Methodist Church. In 1996, he was awarded the Humanitarian Award of the National Conference of Christians and Jews, and in the same year was the recipient of the Clergy of the Year award of the South Coast Ecumenical Council.

Eulogy for James Roosevelt by the Reverend Kenneth E. McMillan

We're here today to honor and celebrate the life of James Roosevelt, and we're here to commend his life to God's eternal love and care which never end.

Jim's life spanned every decade of this twentieth century. He began his life on this earth in New York City on December 23, 1907, the eldest child of Franklin and Eleanor Roosevelt. He entered into life eternal at dawn last Tuesday morning at the age of eighty-three. Jim is survived by his wife, Mary . . . by seven children: Sara, Kate, James, Michael, Anne, Del, and Becky . . . by twenty grandchildren and a number of great-grandchildren.

Jim was very clear that when he died there was to be a simple service . . . not a celebration of his life with presentations by dignitaries and eulogies by celebrities . . . but rather a simple service of the church committing his life into God's eternal care and keeping. And though Hyde Park has been so much a part of the Roosevelt heritage and tradition, it was Jim's choice not to be buried there or to have his service there. He felt that Newport Beach had become his home, his community, and he chose to stay here.

Yes, Jim was a public figure, and the recognition and ceremony are appropriate and important, but Jim was also a private person whose wishes we honor here today. Nonetheless there is much to be said about this man who in a real sense represents the end of an era, the last of an age.

Some of my favorite lines are by that author who calls himself "anonymous," and they go like this: "I shall pass through this world but once. Any good thing, therefore, that I can do, or any kindness I can show to any fellow human being, let me do it now. Let me not defer it nor neglect it, for I shall not pass this way again."

James Roosevelt passed through this world and through our lives and the lives of so many others, and he made a difference because of the special person he was, and all the contributions he made. In the minds of each of you here this afternoon, Jim was an important person in your life. Your presence here to honor and celebrate his life bears witness to that fact. And while it is impossible to put into words all the impact and contributions of Jim's eighty-three years on this earth, yet it is important that we take time to thank God for the variety of relationships and memories and meanings that Jim created with each of us who are gathered here to honor and to celebrate his life.

In one of his books, Jim wrote this about his own life, and that of his sister and three brothers: "It has certainly been an eventful life. I was privileged to have had parents who made history. If that made our lives difficult, it was worth it. For all the problems it imposed upon us, I don't believe any of us would have swapped what we had for uneventful lives in the shadows. I think we all feel we contributed at least a little to the life of this country though much of this century."

And in another place, Jim wrote this about the legacy and heritage of his family name: "It was my greatest asset, no doubt of that. But if it was a plus, it also was a minus. I was not my father. I did have a lot of him in me: I shared much of his philosophy of life and many of his ideals; we wanted the same sorts of things for people; I admired him and supported most of his stands. But I had to be myself."

And he was. James Roosevelt was his own man. And that's the reason so many came to love and admire and appreciate him.

He served his country and the wider human community in a variety of ways and through a myriad of relationships and responsibilities.

During the Second World War he served with distinction in the U.S. Marine Corps as commanding officer of the Fourth Marine Raider Battalion and as executive officer of the Second Marine Raider Battalion. He was awarded the Navy Cross and the Silver Star for gallantry in action. He was a gentle man, but a heroic man who did what he had to do. He was known across the world as Colonel Roosevelt, but in reality he is a retired brigadier general in the U.S. Marine Corps, and it is appropriate that the flags at every Marine facility around the world remain at half-staff until Taps is sounded today in memory and tribute to General James Roosevelt.

Typical of the many words of tribute to Jim are words from retired Marine Corps Lieutenant General William "Gay" Thrash, who wrote: "In spite of his many accomplishments, I always thought of Jim as a Marine.

I first met him at the recruit depot in San Diego in 1940. He did so much for the Marine Corps, both during World War II and after he had left the corps. But I can truthfully say that the Marine Corps is a better corps for having had him serve. He will not be forgotten."

Jim was a politician and statesman . . . politics was in his blood. He was a six-term congressman from California, and served for three years as the U.S. representative to the United Nations Economic and Social Council. In more recent years he served as a member and chair of the Orange County Transportation Commission. His life in politics was not always successful. Jim made losing bids both for the governorship of the state of California and the job of mayor of the city of Los Angeles. But he also acknowledged how much he learned from both those efforts. And in all his political career, he continued to exemplify the high ideals and moral commitment which represent our nation at its best.

Jim was an educator. He lectured at universities and colleges across the land. He helped found the Enterprise Institute at Chapman College and served on the board of trustees of that institution.

He was a consultant and businessman. Again, he was not always successful, and indeed there were some rather notable failures. Jim trusted people and thought they would be fair, and that sometimes caused his downfall. Indeed, in one place he wrote, "Well, which of us is perfect? I am not, certainly. But there are things to be said for me, as well as against me."

So it was. We're here today, not to memorialize a saint, but to pay tribute to a human being who always tried to do his best.

Jim was a humanitarian. He had a passion for social justice, a lifelong concern for the underdog and the oppressed. He was honored as the Humanitarian of the Year by the National Conference of Christians and Jews, and granted the National Americanism award by the Anti-Defamation League of B'nai B'rith.

It was Jim's concern for older people that led him to found the National Committee to Preserve Social Security and Medicare, seeking to carry on and preserve his father's dream.

Jim was a churchman. He was a lifelong member of the Episcopal Church in Hyde Park, but for a long number of years was an affiliate member of this Newport Center UMC, making this an appropriate place for this funeral service.

In 1978 I was asked to come and serve as pastor of this church. I was not really interested in doing that, because things were going well for me in my pastorate in Sierra Madre. Nonetheless, the district superintendent continued to pressure me, and finally came up with the clincher by saying, "And there are many really important, influential people in the

Newport Center church. Why, James Roosevelt, the eldest son of F.D.R., is a member of that church." And my irreverent answer was "Big deal! Ben Wade, chief scout for the Los Angeles Dodgers, is a member of my present church, and I can go to the Dodger games for free whenever I want." After much thought and prayer, I finally did agree to come to this church.

I was privileged to serve as Jim's pastor here for six-and-a-half years. During that time Jim was in morning worship every Sunday. And if he was going to be out of town, he would always bring his offering envelope to the church office, often on his way to the airport on Sunday morning before an early flight. One of the gifts that Jim shared with this church was his periodic presentation about the affairs of the nation and state, particularly before elections. We always appreciated the insight and particular perspective which Jim brought to these talks.

I'm grateful for the support and encouragement Jim and Mary gave me in those years, allowing me to be their pastor. I will always treasure the friendship Jim and Mary have shared with me and my family in the years that have followed my pastorate here. Jim has been a good friend, and I will miss him very much.

Family was important to Jim. He shared warmth and affection with his children, was proud of them, and could often be heard bragging about their accomplishments. His marriage to Mary brought new meaning to Jim's life, and their relationship has been one of warmth and care and stability. More than once Jim told me that Mary was one of the best things to happen to him in his life.

James Roosevelt lived a controversial life. He was not afraid to take a stand about an issue that concerned him. He had a strong mind and will, and unusually sound political instincts. Jim was a public figure who was unflappable; nothing seemed to faze him; he was adaptable to almost every situation.

Jim had a command of world and local affairs. He read extensively in politics and economics. He read the daily newspapers and absorbed them . . . even in these last days. He had friends all over the world, mixed with world leaders and had their admiration and respect. During this past week Mary has had lengthy phone calls from former president Richard Nixon, with whom Jim served years ago in the U.S. House of Representatives . . . and from former president Ronald Reagan whom Jim has known since they worked together in the film industry prior to World War II. . . . Both paid individual tribute to the contribution Jim has made to the people of this nation, and expressed to Mary and the family their love and support.

Jim walked with the mighty, but he also had time and place for ordinary people. He had that gift of making whomever he was dealing with feel valued and important.

Jim had a delightful sense of humor. He was a great storyteller. He loved animals and sailing. He never missed a football game if he could help it. The whole family appropriately went to the Ram's game last night (it was a lousy game) as a way of carrying on that tradition. And I can recall several delightful evenings of going to an Angel's game with Jim.

Jim was a gentle man and a gentleman. He was a warm and genuine person, a concerned and supportive friend, a dedicated and effective public servant, a caring father and a devoted husband, a gracious and caring human being.

The last years of Jim's life have been marked by increasingly ill health . . . Parkinson's disease and a series of strokes. Jim saw all these health problems as a nuisance; he had other things to be about . . . he had a great will and desire to live and to serve. It was hard to see this man of dignity increasingly experience the lack of dignity which comes from hospitals and rest homes.

Special tribute must be paid to Dr. Stanley VanderNoort, who as Jim's personal physician, but more than that, his friend, brought his medical skill and human compassion to make Jim's last years and days more peaceful and comfortable. Jim's mind remained clear even as his body increasingly betrayed him. Just a week ago Friday he conducted a TV interview about Joseph Kennedy.

Jim died peacefully at home . . . that was his strong desire. Dr. VanderNoort had been with him that night. Mary was by his side as he moved into another world just as the dawn of a new day broke.

Jim was increasingly aware of his own mortality. He asked questions about life after death and raised concerns about the mistakes he had made in his life. . . . Would they be held against him? . . . Was the God in whom he believed really a forgiving God? . . . Was there a place for Jim in God's eternal love and care? We talked about that, and Jim was reassured by the promises of his faith, he looked to the future with hope, and he died at peace with himself, with the world around him, and with God.

He died trusting in the words of the apostle Paul that nothing in life or in death can separate us from God and from God's love . . . that there is nothing love cannot face, and that love lasts forever. I believe that with all my heart! And I believe that even now Jim is experiencing God's love in a whole new and deeper dimension, that God is caring for him in a special way, that the God who created us all in the miracle of birth is also the same God who in love receives us all in the mystery of death.

The other day I was at Long Beach Airport, and I saw some words inscribed on a wall. They were written by John McGee, a nineteen-year-old Canadian Air Force pilot, who one day while flying 30,000 feet over the earth, composed these lines:

Oh! I have slipped the surly bonds of earth,
And danced the skies on laughter-silvered wings;
Sunward I've climbed, and joined the tumbling mirth
Of sunlit clouds—and done a hundred things
You have not dreamed of—wheeled and soared and swung
High in the silence. Hov'ring there,
I've chased the shouting wind along, and flung
My eager craft through footless halls of air.

Up, up the long delirious burning blue
I've topped wind-swept heights with easy grace,
Where never lark, or even eagle flew;
And while with silent, lifting mind I've trod
The high untrespassed sanctity of space,
Put out my hand and touched the face of God.

In a real sense Jim has slipped the surly bonds of earth and touched the face of God, and he knows more than any of us about God's care which never ends and God's love which never lets us go.

Jesus put it this way for us, "In my Father's house are many rooms. I go to prepare a place for you, that where I am, you may be also. So let not your hearts be troubled, neither let them be afraid." It is because we believe that promise . . . because we affirm that hope . . . that we are able this day in faith and trust to commit the life of Jim Roosevelt into God's eternal love and care and keeping.

There's an old Irish blessing which goes like this:

May the road rise up to meet you,
May the wind be always at your back,
May the sun shine warm upon your face,
And the rains fall soft upon your fields . . .
And until we meet again,
May God hold you in the palm of his hand.

I believe all of us are held in the palm of God's hand . . . and that now Jim in a special way has gone to be with God forever. So today we give thanks to God for his life, and in confident faith and trust we commend his life to God's eternal love and care which never end.

[Closing prayer] Gracious God, we thank you for all those who have died in the Lord, and who now rest from their labors. Especially we thank you for the life of your servant, James Roosevelt. We are grateful for your guiding hand along the way of his pilgrimage through life. We're thankful for your grace which enabled him to fight the good fight, to endure to the end, to obtain the victory, yes, to become more than conqueror through him who loves us. We're grateful that his spirit is at home in your presence, and that you love him with an infinite unending love. Thank you, God, for surrounding his family with comfort and sustaining courage. Thank you for these friends who come to share in these moments of thanksgiving for his life. Teach us all to face death unafraid, and to know that in everything you are working for good with those who love and trust you, through Jesus Christ our Lord. Amen.

Adlai E. Stevenson

February 5, 1900 ~ July 14, 1965

Eulogy delivered by President Lyndon B. Johnson

Adlai E. Stevenson

American politician and diplomat Adlai Ewing Stevenson II was born in Los Angeles and moved to Illinois with his family at the age of six. He graduated from Princeton University in 1922 and received his law degree from Northwestern University in Illinois in 1926. After spending two years editing a family newspaper, he took up the practice of law in Chicago.

In 1941, Stevenson went to Washington as attorney for Navy Secretary Frank Knox, and in 1945 became a special assistant to Secretary of State Edward Stettinus Jr. Until 1947, he served as an aide to the American delegation to the General Assembly of the United Nations Organization. He returned to Chicago in 1948 and was elected governor of Illinois, heading an administration noted for its efficiency and lack of corruption.

Stevenson stood against Dwight D. Eisenhower as the Democratic presidential candidate in both 1952 and 1956, but each time his urbane "egg-headed" campaign speeches had more appeal abroad than at home. In 1954, he published *A Call to Greatness*. He returned to his Chicago law practice in 1957, and in 1961 President John F. Kennedy appointed him the U.S. ambassador to the United Nations. Serving until 1965, he played a role in such historical events as the Bay of Pigs invasion, the Cuban missile crisis, and the conflict in Vietnam.

Lyndon B. Johnson

For a biographical sketch, see the eulogy for Lyndon B. Johnson, page 62. Lyndon Johnson delivered the eulogy during the first year of his presidency.

Eulogy for Adlai E. Stevenson by Lyndon B. Johnson

The flame which illuminated the dreams and expectations of an entire world is now extinguished. Adlai Stevenson of Illinois is dead.

His great hero, Abraham Lincoln, said at the beginning of his political career that "I have no other (ambition) so great as that of being truly esteemed of my fellowmen, by rendering myself worthy of their esteem."

And although his disappointments were many, in this, like Lincoln, he was vindicated.

Like Lincoln he was rooted in America's heartland, yet his voice reached across every boundary of nation and race and class.

Like Lincoln he was a great emancipator. It was his gift to help emancipate men from narrowness of mind and the shackles which selfishness and ignorance place upon the human adventure.

Like Lincoln he will be remembered more for what he stood for than for the offices he held; more for the ideals he embodied than for the positions in which he served. For history honors men more for what they were than who they were. And by this standard he holds a permanent place on that tiny roster of those who will be remembered as long as mankind is strong enough to honor greatness.

It seems such a short time ago that, out of Illinois, came that thoughtful eloquence summoning an entire nation back from its dangerous drift toward contentment and complacency. For an entire generation of Americans he imparted a nobility to public life and a grandeur to American purpose which has already reshaped the life of the nation and which will endure for many generations.

One by one he sounded the great themes of our time—peace and justice and the well-being of humanity. And many men will labor for many years toward the vision and high purpose which was the gorgeously crafted outpouring of this man's heart and skills.

He was an American. And he served his country well. But what he saw, and what he spoke, and what he worked for, is the shared desire of humanity. He believed in us, perhaps more than we deserved. And so we came to believe in ourselves, more than we had. And if we persevere, then, on the foundation of that faith we can build the wondrous works of peace and of justice among the nations.

He will not see that day. But it will be his day still.

Let us therefore, adversary and friend alike, pause for a moment and weep for one who was a friend and guide to all mankind.

Danny Thomas

January 6, 1912 ~ February 5, 1991

Tribute by Congressman Nick Rahall II given in Congress on February 5, 1991, and appearing as part of the *Congressional Record*

Danny Thomas

Television star and philanthropist Danny Thomas (originally Muzyad Yakhoob, later Amos Jacobs) was born of Lebanese immigrant parents in Deerfield, Michigan. He married Rose Marie Cassaniti in 1936. Their three children include actress Marlo Thomas.

Beginning his career in radio during the 1930s, he changed his name to Danny Thomas in 1940 when he began work as a nightclub comedian. In the early forties he appeared on Fanny Brice's radio show, and from 1944 to 1949 had his own program, "The Danny Thomas Show." Thomas also made several movies, including *Call Me Mister* (1951) and *The Jazz Singer* (1953).

In 1953, Thomas moved to television to star in his series, *Make Room for Daddy,* which won five Emmys. He also was a television producer, and was responsible for such successes as *The Andy Griffith Show, The Dick Van Dyke Show,* and *The Mod Squad.* He continued to make television appearances throughout the 1970s and 1980s.

Thomas was an untiring fund-raiser for his cause, the St. Jude Children's Research Hospital, which he founded in 1962. He was honored by such organizations as the National Conference of Christians and Jews and the American Medical Association.

Nick Rahall II

Congressman Nick Joe Rahall II was born in Beckley, West Virginia, on May 20, 1949, the son of Joe and Alice Rahall. He received his A.B. from Duke University in 1971, and served as a staff assistant to U.S. Senator Robert C. Byrd from 1971 to 1974. Rahall has been a member of Congress since 1977 as a representative from the Fourth (now the Third) West Virginia District.

Tribute for Danny Thomas by Nick Rahall II

Like most of America, I heard the sad news on the way to work this morning of the passing of the beloved comedian Danny Thomas.

Danny Thomas, an individual of Lebanese extraction, was presented the Congressional Gold Medal by the U.S. Congress in 1983. I introduced that legislation on January 3 of that year with the immeasurable help of my esteemed colleague from Illinois (Mr. Annunzio), and with 225 cosponsors we passed that resolution and President Reagan then presented the gold medal to Danny Thomas in the White House on April 16, 1985.

At that time President Reagan spoke of Danny Thomas's remarkable career in acting. His career, however, was overshadowed and paled in comparison with his true achievement, which was his work in founding and setting up St. Jude's Children's Research Hospital.

Danny Thomas fulfilled a promise he made when he was a struggling young comedian to St. Jude, the patron saint of the hopeless, when he vowed to build a shrine to St. Jude should he become a success in show business. He became that success, and in 1946 he raised the needed funds for the St. Jude's Children's Research Hospital in Memphis, Tennessee. He established the American-Lebanese-Syrian Associated Charities to undertake this fund-raising effort for the hospital. The work paid off, and in 1962 St. Jude's Children's Research Hospital opened its doors, making Danny's dream of free medical care for children a reality. And largely through Danny's tireless efforts, today St. Jude's has more than doubled the size of its patient and research facilities. Over the years it has treated more than five thousand young patients. The care and love that are given to the children of this world at St. Jude's is second to none. It reflects the character and dedication of its benefactor, Danny Thomas.

St. Jude's has achieved a remarkable 53 percent cure rate for children suffering from leukemia, a tribute to the dedicated staff at the hospital.

So today, Mr. Speaker, I conclude in joining with the world as we mourn the loss of a truly beloved American, a comedian, but more important than that, a friend, and a true carer for all the children of the world.

Orson Welles

May 6, 1915 ~ October 10, 1985

Eulogy delivered by Charlton Heston at a memorial service, The Directors' Guild, Los Angeles, California

Orson Welles

American actor and director George Orson Welles was born in Kenosha, Wisconsin, to a wealthy, cultured family. Declared a child prodigy, his only formal education was five years at a private school, which he entered at age ten. Welles married three times, and had a daughter from each marriage.

In the early 1930s, Welles made his acting debut at the age of sixteen in Dublin, Ireland. He returned to the United States in the mid-thirties to continue his stage career, making his Broadway debut in a 1934 production of *Romeo and Juliet.*

Turning his attention to radio, Welles became the distinctive voice of Lamont Cranston on the popular series "The Shadow." In 1938, his Mercury Theatre company staged an on-air version of H. G. Wells's *War of the Worlds,* causing near panic among listeners over its reports of Martian landings.

Welles moved to Hollywood in 1940, and in 1941 released *Citizen Kane,* famous for its innovations in photography, camera work, and film editing. His subsequent, less critically acclaimed films include *The Third Man* (1949), *Othello* (1952), and *Touch of Evil* (1958).

While he continued to write and direct for both the film and television industries, Welles's enormous, early successes were never repeated. In his later years, his achievements as an artist were honored by such organizations as the American Film Institute and the Directors' Guild of America.

Charlton Heston

Stage and screen actor Charlton Heston (originally John Charlton Carter) was born on October 4, 1924, the son of Russell Whitford and Lilla (Charlton) Carter. He married Lydia Marie Clarke in 1944.

Heston's stage performances have included *Antony and Cleopatra,* and he has made many television appearances, including *Macbeth, Treasure Island,* and *The Colbys*. His many films include *The Greatest Show on Earth* (1952), *The Naked Jungle* (1954), *The Ten Commandments* (1956), *Ben Hur* (1959), *Planet of the Apes* (1969), *The Omega Man* (1971), and *Midway* (1976). He also directed and starred in the 1982 production *Mother Lode*.

Heston is a trustee of the Los Angeles Center Theatre Group, and was its chairman in 1973. Since 1978, he has been a member of the American Academy of Motion Picture Arts and Sciences, and is also a member of the Screen Actors Guild, for which he served as president from 1966 to 1971.

Eulogy for Orson Welles by Charlton Heston

One of the luckiest things that ever happened to me in my career, I think, was the chance to work with Orson Welles in *Touch of Evil*. It was an extraordinary experience, and an enormously valuable lesson in film. He taught me all kinds of things: about how important it is for actors with bass voices to use their tenor range; he was the first man to ever take me into a cutting room, which he did with great generosity and great patience. He also was the most entertaining director I've ever worked for. People imagine filmmaking is a lot of fun. They say, "Oh it must have been marvelous fun to work with so and so, to do that, to be there." Not true. Filmmaking is very hard work, very long days filled with frustration and failure on every hand. You often face a bitter truth: to see yourself falling a little short.

With Orson, somehow, this was not so. It was always exciting—almost a party. "Celebration" is better—it was a celebration. Also, he could do something else. Even in a marvelous part, most of the scenes are not marvelous. Many of the shots are just structural shots. Orson could persuade you that a shot where you drove up and got out of a car and went up a flight of stairs and in a door just happened to be the most important shot in the entire film.

I don't know if he was the best director that ever lived—I suppose he wasn't the best actor. He was an enormously gifted writer, director, producer, actor. I do know that he was the most talented man I ever worked with, indeed ever saw. Talent is a very slippery word in itself—suppose what it means is that smoky, subjective something hidden somewhere inside us allows us to make up plays and paintings and bridges and airplanes and murals . . . and movies. Orson had more of that than anyone

I've ever known. Indeed, he was so enormously gifted that these things come from him casually, quite often under pressure—such sudden leaps of the imagination—of the creative intelligence—in moments of absolute panic, that I think that unconsciously he may have created these situations. I think it may be, truly, that maybe throughout his career he subconsciously painted himself into corners just to see how he could get out of them. This, of course, created a sense of wary skepticism in those for whom he worked. And especially in those to whom he had to turn for money. Unhappily, Orson always denied the basic fact of filmmaking—that the raw materials are so expensive that we cannot afford to buy them for ourselves; we must get them from people who have the money, and they want it back; and that's fair.

The only people Orson never would bother to charm (and he could charm anyone) were studio heads. And those are the people who have the money. Which is one of the reasons we have so few pictures from him. We have what is arguably the greatest picture of all, *Citizen Kane*. Peter was very generous about *Touch of Evil,* which I think was more accurately described by *Cahier du Cinema* as "the best 'B' movie ever made." That in itself is a reflection of the ambiguous skepticism with which the film community regarded Orson. But we are lucky to have the films we have. It is our grievous loss that we haven't more of them.

As epitaph, I want to speak a few words from a play we both did many times, *Julius Caesar*. I played Antony, he played Brutus—to my great loss, never together. But it seems to speak some of the things I feel. It also, I think, may have suggested a line he wrote for Marlene Dietrich about his character in *Touch of Evil*. All these are ambiguities of the kind that amused Orson enormously:

> He was my friend, faithful and just to me,
> but Brutus says he was ambitious.
> If it were so, it were a grievous fault
> and grievously hath Caesar answered it.
> He was the noblest Roman of them all,
> the elements so mixed in him that nature
> must stand up and say to all the world,
> "This was a man."

Thank you.

Mae West

August 17, 1893 ~ November 20, 1980

Tribute delivered by Herbert Kenwith

Mae West

Actress Mae West was born in Brooklyn and made her stage debut in 1900 as a child performer. She spent many years in vaudeville and was a success on Broadway before her first film, *Night after Night* (1932). In 1933 she starred in two films, *She Done Him Wrong* and *I'm No Angel.* Throughout the 1930s, a series of racy comedies exploited her voluptuousness and sexual badinage. Although under pressure from the censors, she continued to make films, including the popular 1940 release *My Little Chickadee,* with W. C. Fields.

West returned to the stage and nightclubs, but made two late character appearances in the films *Myra Breckenridge* (1970) and *Sextette* (1978) before her death from a stroke in Los Angeles.

Herbert Kenwith

Producer Herbert Kenwith started his career as an actor and appeared in several Broadway productions. His last Broadway appearance was in *I Remember Mama* with Marlon Brando.

The first theatrical play Kenwith produced and directed was *Night Must Fall* with Dame May Whitty. He was the producer and director of a summer drama festival at Princeton, which ran for six years.

Kenwith was Broadway's youngest producer with his successful production of *Me and Molly.* He later produced and directed a road tour of *There Goes the Bride* starring Gloria Swanson and Robert Alda, as well as the Mae West production tour *Come on Up—Ring Twice!*

Kenwith moved to television as an associate director for CBS, and was assigned such productions as *Lamp unto My Feet* and *Suspicion.* Joining NBC, he directed 750 episodes of *The Doctors* before leaving for Hollywood to direct such popular shows as *Death Valley Days, Name of the Game, Marcus Welby,* and *Star Trek.*

In all, Kenwith has directed (or produced/directed) over two thousand television shows and fifteen hundred commercials.

Mr. Kenwith worked with Ms. West and was one of her close friends for many years.

Tribute for Mae West by Herbert Kenwith

You may think it strange . . . but the truth of the matter is that what Mae West said, "Come up and see me sometime," still applies—perhaps even more so! The characters she created and played may or may not have seemed sufficiently righteous . . . but the human being that Mae West was . . . was . . . and heavenly, too.

So, she's there. With the great stars, and still offering love to one and all.

So . . . Yes . . . when you're ready, "Come up and see her sometime."

Natalie Wood

July 20, 1938 ~ November 30, 1981

Eulogy delivered by Roddy McDowall,
December 2, 1981

Natalie Wood

Born Natasha Gurdin to Russian immigrant parents, American actress Natalie Wood was only one of a handful of Hollywood child stars to successfully make the transition to adult film roles. She was married to actor Robert Wagner in 1957, divorced him in 1963, and then remarried him in 1972. In between, she married Richard Gregson, with whom she had a daughter; the second Wagner marriage also produced a daughter.

Wood's role in *Miracle on 34th Street* in 1947 won critical acclaim for the nine-year-old, and at age seventeen she was nominated for an Academy Award for her performance in *Rebel without a Cause* (1955). She received a second nomination in 1961 for her role in *Splendor in the Grass,* and appeared as Maria in *West Side Story* that same year. In 1963, her performance in *Love with a Proper Stranger* earned her a third Academy Award nomination.

Natalie Wood died at age forty-three from an accidental drowning in the waters off Santa Catalina, California.

Roddy McDowall

Actor Roddy McDowall was born in London on September 28, 1928, the son of Thomas Andrew and Winifred McDowall. He was educated at St. Joseph's School, London.

McDowall's films include *How Green Was My Valley* (1941), *My Friend Flicka* (1943), *Macbeth* (1948), *The Longest Day* (1962), *Planet of the Apes* (1968), and *The Big Picture* (1989).

McDowall's Broadway appearances include *Misalliance, Doctor's Dilemma, No Time for Sergeants, Compulsion,* and *Camelot*. He has made numerous television appearances on *Macmillian and Wife,* and his made-for-television films include *Hart to Hart* (1979), *The Martian Chronicles* (1980), *Mae West* (1982), and *This Girl for Hire* (1983).

McDowall is the author of the books *Double Exposure* and *Take Two,* both published in 1989, and was the recipient of the 1960 Emmy award for best supporting actor. He died in his home, in October 1998, from cancer.

Mr. McDowall was a longtime close friend of Ms. Wood and her family.

Eulogy for Natalie Wood by Roddy McDowell

It is amazing!

I mean, all of us here are merely a tiny part of a virtual multitude of lives that have been blessed in perpetuity because we have known Natalie and darling R. J.

It is awesome . . . actually, it is downright joyous . . . to think that one pretty individual accomplished so much of beauty in so few decades and arrived at a plateau of such personal fulfillment. Why, she found a way to not only put life in her art but art into her life.

She *found* a way to use all her pain, all her demons . . . to *channel* them into understanding, wisdom, compassion, humor, love, and productivity toward *other* lives. And she worked with such diligence to reach that goal and therefore *was* capable of *truly* giving with adult delight and childlike naughtiness.

Natalie, and that prince of all fellows, R. J., have made us all feel so necessary. They have made each of us feel so genuinely important. Made us feel that *we* are capable of wonder.

And Natalie has done it with such a dear delicate will of steel . . . coupled with that adorable infectious giggle . . . and that irresistible trait of "never copping a plea."

I know she will never be gone: I *know* she will never be absent from any one of us . . . because she has left *to* us all . . . and especially to her stunning children . . . she has left us all a legacy that can only strengthen the lives of ANY ONE who HEARD her. If we WISH to employ it, she has given us a slice of vibrant serenity: an invitation to do unto each other as she has done unto us . . . which is only the best.

After all these lovely years of knowing her it seems to me that Natalie is the embodiment of thirty-six words written by William Saroyan: "In the TIME of your life, *live,* so that in wondrous time YOU shall not add to the misery and sorrow of the world . . . but shall smile TO the infinite delight and mystery of it."

And so!

God Bless us all.

And let us be good to each other!

Natalie wanted it that way!

Malcolm X

May 19, 1925 ~ February 21, 1965

Eulogy delivered by Ossie Davis at a memorial service, Harlem, New York

Malcolm X

The American black nationalist leader Malcolm X was born Malcolm Little in Omaha, Nebraska, the son of a radical Baptist minister. By age sixteen, he was in New York City, where he became involved in Harlem's underworld. Imprisoned for burglary from 1946 to 1952, while still in jail he converted to the Black Muslim movement led by Elijah Muhammad. On his release in 1953, he assumed the name Malcolm X, and traveled the country promoting the sect's teachings. An opponent of the integrationist movement, he pressed for black separatism and advocated the use of violence in self-defense.

In 1964, following a trip to Mecca, his views changed and he founded the Organization of Afro-American Unity, which blended elements of orthodox Islam, African socialism, anticolonialism, and racial solidarity. A factional feud ensued, culminating in Malcolm X's assassination by Black Muslim enemies during a Harlem rally in 1965. His ideas were published in 1965 in *The Autobiography of Malcolm X* by Alex Haley.

Ossie Davis

Actor and author Ossie Davis was born in Cogdell, Georgia, on December 18, 1917, the son of Kince Charles and Laura (Cooper) Davis. He married Ruby Ann Wallace (Ruby Dee) in 1948, and the couple had three children. Davis was a student at Howard University from 1935 to 1938. In 1939 he made his stage debut with the Rose McClendoh Players in Harlem; his Broadway debut was in *Jeb* in 1946.

Davis's theater appearances include *A Raisin in the Sun, Purlie Victorious, I'm Not Rappaport* (1987), and *Two Hah-Hahs and a Homeboy* (1995). Davis directed various films, including *Cotton Comes to Harlem* (1970), *Black Girl* (1972), and *Gordon's War* (1973). He was a featured actor in many films, including *The Scalphunters* (1968), *School Daze* (1968), *Do the Right Thing* (in 1989, for which he won a best supporting actor oscar and the NAACP Image Award for his role, DA Mayor), *Malcolm X* (1992), *Grumpy Old Men* (1994), and *The Client* (1994). In addition, he appeared in the television series *B.L. Stryker* and *Evening Shade* (both of which ran from 1990 to 1994).

Davis is the author of *Escape to Freedom: The Story of Young Frederick Douglass* (1978), *Langston* (1982), and *Purlie Victorious* and *Just Like Martin* (both 1992). He was named to the NAACP Image Awards Hall of Fame in 1989, and in 1994 he was inducted into the Theater Hall of Fame.

Eulogy for Malcolm X by Ossie Davis

Here, at this final hour, in this quiet place, Harlem has come to bid farewell to one of its brightest hopes—extinguished now and gone from us forever.

For Harlem is where he worked and where he struggled and fought—his home of homes; where his heart was, and where his people are—and it is, therefore, most fitting that we meet once again—in Harlem—to share these last moments with him.

For Harlem has been ever gracious to those who have loved her, have fought for her, and have defended her honor even to the death. It is not in the memory of man that this beleaguered, unfortunate, but nonetheless proud, community has found a braver, more gallant young champion than this Afro-American who lies before us—unconquered still.

I say the word again, as he would want me to: Afro-American; Afro-American Malcolm, who was a master, was most meticulous in his use of words. Nobody knew better than he the power words have over the minds of men. Malcolm had stopped being "Negro" years ago.

It had become too small, too puny, too weak a word for him. Malcolm was bigger than that. Malcolm had become an Afro-American, and he wanted—so desperately—that we, that all his people would become Afro-Americans, too.

There are those who still consider it their duty, as friends of the Negro people, to tell us to revile him, to flee, even from the presence of his memory, to save ourselves by writing him out of the history of our turbulent times.

Many will ask what Harlem finds to honor in this stormy, controversial and bold young captain. And we will smile.

Many will say turn away, away from this man, for he is not a man but a demon, a monster, a subverter, and an enemy of the black man. And we will smile.

They will say that he is of hate—a fanatic, a racist who can only bring evil to the cause for which you struggle.

And we will answer and say unto them: did you ever talk to Brother Malcolm? Did you ever touch him, or have him smile at you? Did you ever really listen to him? Did he ever do a mean thing? Was he ever himself associated with violence or any public disturbance? For if you did, you would know him. And if you knew him, you would know why we must honor him.

Malcolm was our manhood, our living Black manhood! This was his meaning to his people. And, in honoring him, we honor the best in ourselves.

Last year, from Africa, he wrote these words to a friend: "My journey (he says) is almost ended, and I have a much broader scope than when I started out, which I believe will add new life and dimension to our struggle for freedom and honor, and dignity in the States. I'm writing these things so that you will know for a fact the tremendous sympathy and support we have among the African States for our human-rights struggle. The main thing is that we keep a united front wherein our most valuable time and energy will not be wasted fighting each other."

However much we may have differed with him—or with each other about him and his value as a man—let his going from us serve only to bring us together now. Consigning these mortal remains to earth, the common mother of all, secure in the knowledge that what we place in the ground is no more now a man, but a seed, which, after the winter of discontent, will come forth again to meet us. And we shall know him then for what he was and is—a prince, our own black shining prince, who didn't hesitate to die, because he loved us so.

Appendix

Deceased	Eulogist
Armstrong, Louis (7/4/1900–7/6/71)	Charles B. Rangel
Ashe, Arthur (7/10/43–2/6/93)	L. Douglas Wilder
Burns, George (1/20/1896–3/9/96)	Irving Fein
Chavez, Cesar (3/31/27–4/23/93)	Cardinal Roger Mahony
Churchill, Sir Winston (11/30/1874–1/24/65)	Dwight D. Eisenhower
Connally, John (2/27/17–6/15/93)	Lady Bird Johnson
Disney, Walt (12/5/01–12/15/66)	Roy O. Disney
Eisenhower, Dwight D. (10/14/1890–3/28/69)	Richard Nixon
Fonda, Henry (5/16/05–8/12/82)	Max Baucus
Ford, Henry (7/30/1863–4/7/47)	Edgar A. Guest
Frost, Robert (3/26/1874–1/29/63)	John F. Kennedy
Gonzales, Pancho (5/9/28–7/3/95)	Bud Collins
Hayes, Helen (10/10/1900–3/17/93)	Cliff Robertson
Hubbell, Carl (6/22/03–11/21/88)	Vernon Markwell
Javits, Jacob (5/18/04–3/7/86)	Daniel P. Moynihan

Johnson, Lyndon B. (8/27/08–1/22/73)	Dean Rusk
Kennedy, John F. (5/29/17–11/22/63)	Jacob Javits
Kennedy, Robert (11/20/28–6/6/68)	Edward Kennedy
King, Martin Luther, Jr. (1/15/29–4/4/68)	Benjamin E. Mays
Kunstler, William (7/7/19–9/4/95)	Ronald L. Kuby
Laurel, Stan (6/16/1890–2/23/65)	Dick Van Dyke
Lazar, Irving Paul (3/28/07–12/30/93)	Larry McMurtry
Mantle, Mickey (10/20/31–8/13/95)	Bob Costas
Marshall, George C. (12/31/1880–10/16/59)	Frank McCarthy
Marshall, Thurgood (7/2/08–1/24/93)	William H. Rehnquist
Mulligan, Gerry (4/6/27–1/20/96)	Dave Brubeck
Muskie, Edmund (3/28/14–3/26/96)	Jimmy Carter
Niven, David (3/1/10–7/29/83)	William F. Buckley
Nixon, Richard M. (1/9/13–4/22/94)	Bill Clinton
O'Connell, Helen (5/23/20–9/9/93)	Turnley Walker
Pauling, Linus (2/28/01–8/19/94)	Frank Catchpool
Peale, Norman Vincent (5/31/1898–12/24/93)	Margaret Peale Everett
Rabin, Yitzhak (3/1/22–11/4/95)	King Hussein
Rayburn, Sam (1/6/1882–11/16/61)	James Roosevelt
Roosevelt, Eleanor (10/12/1882–11/7/62)	Adlai E. Stevenson
Roosevelt, James (12/23/07–8/13/91)	Kenneth E. McMillan

Stevenson, Adlai E. (2/5/1900–7/14/65)	Lyndon B. Johnson
Thomas, Danny (1/6/12–2/5/91)	Nick Rahall II
Welles, Orson (5/6/15–10/10/85)	Charlton Heston
West, Mae (8/17/1893–11/20/80)	Herbert Kenwith
Wood, Natalie (7/20/38–11/30/81)	Roddy McDowall
X, Malcolm (5/19/25–2/21/65)	Ossie Davis

Eulogist Index

Eulogized Index
(by subject area)

Arts

Business

Entertainment

Government, Politics

Professional

Religious

Sports

About the Author

Born in New York City in 1932, Ted Tobias spent the first twenty-eight years of his life in the South Bronx and the past forty years on the West Coast, primarily in Beverly Hills, California. He graduated from the City College of New York, uptown, and later spent two years in graduate social work study at Hunter College. To earn money for school, he sandwiched in a five-year stint as an NBC page. On the West Coast, Tobias has been a successful entrepreneur, whose interests ranged from computer software development to television, stage, and motion picture production. He also operated a well-known seven-store retail chain dealing in art supplies and fine pens for over thirty years. A widower since 1999, Tobias resides in Beverly Hills. He is currently penning a memoir of his happy marriage of forty years and the three months of his wife's terminal illness. In Tribute II will be published in mid-2002.